SECRETS OF ACCESS DATABASE DEVELOPMENT AND PROGRAMMING!

By

ANDREI BESEDIN

Copyright © 2017

TABLE OF CONTENTS

LEGAL NOTES AND DISCLAIMER

CHAPTER 1. TABLES

Introduction to tables

- Tables are essential objects in a database; they hold all the information or data
- Each table stores data about a particular subject, such as employees or products.
- A table has records (rows) and fields (columns).
- Fields have different types of data, such as text, numbers, dates, and hyperlinks.
- A record: Contains specific data, like information about a particular employee or product.
- A field Contains data about one aspect of the table subject, such as first name or e-mail address.
- A field value: Each record has a field value.

To connect the data stored in different tables, you would create relationships. A relationship is a logical connection between two tables that have a standard field.

Keys

Fields that are part of a table relationship are called keys. A key usually consists of one field, but may include more than one field.

There are two kinds of keys:

- Primary key: A table can have only one primary key. A primary key consists of one or more fields that uniquely identify each record that you store in the table. Access automatically provides a unique identification number, called an ID number that serves as a primary key.
- Foreign key: A table can have one or more external keys. A foreign key contains values that correspond to values in the primary key of another table. For example, you might have an orders table in which each order has a customer ID number that corresponds to a record in a Customers table. The customer ID field is a foreign key of the Orders table.

BENEFITS OF USING RELATIONSHIPS

- **Consistency.** Each item of data is recorded only once, in one table, there is less opportunity for inconsistency.
- **Efficiency.**Recording data in only one place means you use less disk space.

- **Comprehensibility.** The design of a database is easier to understand if the subjects are adequately separated into tables.

Create a new table in a new desktop database

1. Under **File**, click **New** > **Blank desktop database**.
2. In the **File Name** box, type a file name for the new database.
3. To save the database in a different location, click the folder icon.
4. Click **Create**.

   The new database opens, with a new table named Table1, rename the table based on the type of data stored in it.

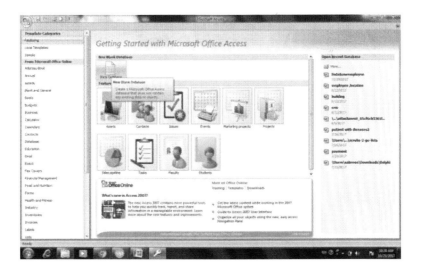

Create a new table in an existing database

1. Click **File >Open**, and click the database if it is listed under **Recent**. If not, select one of the browse options to locate the database.
2. Under **Create**, click **Table**.

   A new table is added and opens in Datasheet view.

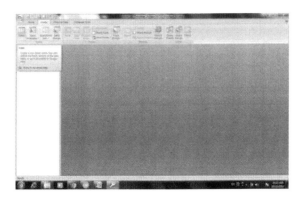

Names of fields, controls, and objects in Microsoft Access desktop databases:

- It can be up to 64 characters long.
- It can include any combination of letters, numbers, spaces, and special characters except a period (.), an exclamation point (!), an accent grave (`), and brackets ([ ]).
- It cannot begin with leading spaces.
- It cannot include control characters (ASCII values 0 through 31).
- It cannot include a double quotation mark (") in table, view, or stored procedure names in a Microsoft Access project.

Add a field automatically by entering data

1. Open the table to which you want to add a field.
2. Type your data into the cell below the **Click to 'Add'** column header.

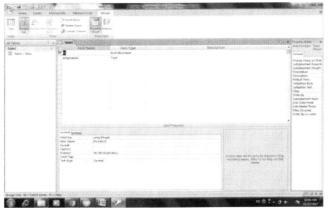

Add a field (column) in the middle of a table

1. Open the table in Datasheet view.
2. Select the field in front of the position where you want to add a new field. For example, if you want the newfield to be the third field in the table, select the second field.
3. Right click, then choose insert column.

-You can change various aspects of a field after you create it, but fielddoes not have data to make rename.

-To rename a field, double-click the field label, and then type the new name.

-To move a field, right click on field then double click on delete column.

Set the field size

-You can change the field size of a field that is empty or that already contains data. The effect of changing the field size depends on whether the field already includes data.

- **If the field does not contain data.**When you change the field size, the size of new data values is limited for the field. For number fields, the field size determines precisely how much disk space Access uses for each value of the field. For text fields, the field size specifies the maximum amount of disk space that Access allows for each value of the field.
- **If the field contains data.**When you change the field size, Access truncates all the values in the field that exceeds the specified field size and also limits the size of new data values for the field.

<u>Example</u>

1. In the Navigation Pane, right-click the table that contains the field that you want to change, and then click **Design View**.
2. In the table design grid, select the field for which you want to change the field size.
3. In the **Field Properties** pane, on the **General** tab, enter the new field size in the **Field Size** property.
4. You can choose from the following values:

   - **Byte**: For integers that range from 0 to 255. Storage requirement is a single byte.
   - **Integer**: For integers that range from -32,768 to +32,767. Storage requirement is two bytes.
   - **Long Integer**: For integers that range from -2,147,483,648 to +2,147,483,647. Storage requirement is four bytes.
   - **Single**: For numeric floating point values that range from -3.4 x 1038 to +3.4 x 1038 and up to seven significant digits. Storage requirement is four bytes.
   - **Double**: For numeric floating point values that range from -1.797 x 10308 to +1.797 x 10308 and up to 15 significant digits. Storage requirement is eight bytes.
   - **Replication ID**: For storing a GUID that is required for replication. Storage requirement is 16 bytes.

- **Decimal**: For numeric values that range from -9.999... × 1027 to + 9.999... × 1027. Storage requirement is 12 bytes.

-You can also change field size in thetext.

- In the Navigation Pane, right-click the table that contains the field that you want to change, and then click **Design View**.
- In the table design grid, select the field for which you want to change the field size.
- In the **Field Properties** pane, on the **General** tab, enter the new field size in the **Field Size** property. You can enter a value from 1 to 255.

Create a calculated field in table datasheet

1. Open the table by double-clicking it in the Navigation Pane.
2. Scroll horizontally to the rightmost column in the table, and click the **Click to 'Add'** 'column heading.
3. In the list that appears, click **Calculated Field**, and then click the data type that you want for the result, Access displays the Expression Builder.
4. Begin typing the calculation that you want for this field, for example:

   [Quantity] * [Unit Price]

5. Click **OK**.
6. Type a name for the calculated field, and then press ENTER.

Modify calculated field in datasheet

- Open the table by double-clicking it in the Navigation Pane.
- Click on the calculated field that you want to modify.

- On the **Fields** tab, in the **Properties** group, click **Modify Expression**.
- In the expression box, make the necessary modifications to the calculation.
- Click OK.

Add an input mask to a Table Field using the Input Mask Wizard

You can use input masks with fields that are set to the Text, Number, Currency, and Date/Time data types.

1. In the Navigation Pane, right-click the table and click **Design View** on the shortcut menu.
2. Click the field where you want to add the input mask.
3. Under **Field Properties**, on the **General** tab, click the **Input Mask** property box.
4. Click the **Build** button to start the Input Mask Wizard.
5. In the Input Mask list, select the type of mask that you want to add.

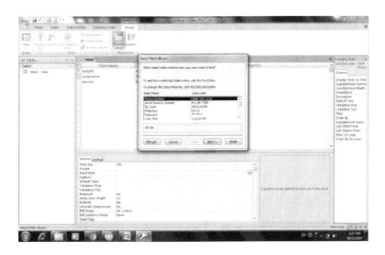

6. Click **Try it** and enter data to test how the mask displays.
7. To keep the input mask without any changes, click **Next**.
8. Select an option for how you want the data to be stored.
9. Click **Finish** and save your changes.

Add an input mask to a query

1. In the Navigation Pane, right-click the query that you want to change and click **Design View** on the shortcut menu.
2. In the query design grid, place the pointer in the column for the field you want to change, you can place the cursor in any row for that field.
3. Press F4 to open the property sheet for the field.
4. Under **Field Properties**, on the **General** tab, click the **Input Mask** property box.
5. Click the **Build** button, to start the Input Mask Wizard, and then follow the instructions in the wizard.

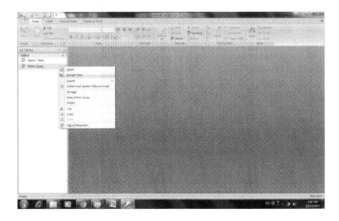

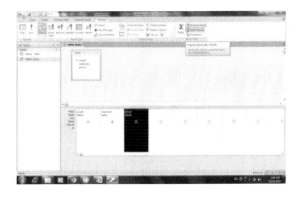

6.

<u>Add an input mask to a form or report control</u>

1. In the Navigation Pane, right-click the form or report that you want to change and click **Design View** on the shortcut menu.
2. Right-click the control that you want to change, and then click **Properties** on the shortcut menu.
3. On the **All** tab, click the **Input Mask** property box.
4. Click the **Build** button to start the Input Mask Wizard, and then follow the instructions in the wizard.

5.

CUSTOMIZE INPUT MASKS FROM THE INPUT MASK WIZARD

1. Open the object in Design View, and click the field where you want to add the custom input mask.
2. Click the **Build** to start the Input Mask Wizard.
3. Click **Edit List**.
4. The **Customize Input Mask Wizard** dialog box appears.

5. Move to a new record in the dialog and enter a new description in the **Description** text box.
6. In the **Input Mask**, text box enters characters and placeholders using the allowed characters from the tablelist.
7. Click the **Mask Type** down arrow and select a suitable mask type.
8. Click **Close**. The new input mask displays in the list.

-You can also use the **Validation Rule** property to require specific values, and the **Validation Text** property to alert your users to any mistakes. For example, entering a rule such as **>100 And<1000** in the **Validation Rule** property enforce users to enter values between 100 and 1,000. A rule such as **[EndDate]>=[StartDate]** forces users to enter an ending date that occurs on or after a starting date. Entering text such as "Enter values between 100 and 1,000" or "Enter an ending date on or after the start date" in the **Validation Text** property tells users when they have made a mistake and how to fix the error.

- **Input masks.**You can use an input mask to validate data by forcing users to enter values in a specific way. For example, an input mask can force users to enter dates in a European format, such as 2007.04.14.

Types of validation rules

You can create two basic types of validation rules:

- **Field validation rules** Use a field validation rule to check the value that you enter in a field when you leave the field. For example, suppose you have a Date field, and you enter **>=#01/01/2010#** in the **Validation Rule** property of that field. Your rule now requires users to enter dates on or after January 1, 2010. If you entera date earlier than 2010 and then try to place the focus on another field, Access prevents you from leaving the current field until you fix the problem.

- **Record validation rules** Use a record validation rule to control when you can save a record (a row in a table). Unlike a field validation rule, a record validation rule refers to other fields in the same table. You create record validation rules when you need to check the values in one field against the values

Create a field validation rule

1. Select the field that you want to validate.
2. On the **Fields** tab, in the **Field Validation** group, click **Validation**, and then click **Field Validation Rule**.
3. Use the Expression Builder to create the rule.

Create a message to display for field input that is not valid

1. Select the field that needs a message for input that is not valid. The field should already have a validation rule.
2. On the **Fields** tab, in the **Field Validation** group, click **Validation**, and then click **Field Validation Message**.
3. Enter an appropriate message. For example, if the validation rule is **>10, the word might be "Enter a value that is less than 10."**

Create a record validation rule

1. Open the table for which you want to validate records.
2. On the **Fields** tab, in the **Field Validation** group, click **Validation**, and then click **Record Validation Rule**.
3. Use the Expression Builder to create the rule.

Test existing data against a new validation rule

-If you add a validation rule to an existing table, you might want to test the rule to see whether any current data is not valid.

1. Open the table that you want to test in Design View.

   On the **Design** tab, in the **Tools** group, click **Test Validation Rules**.

2. Click **Yes** to close the alert message and start the test.
3. If prompted to save your table, click **Yes**.

   CREATE A VALIDATION RULE FOR A CONTROL

1. Right-click the form that you want to change, and then click **Layout View**.
2. Right-click the control that you want to change, and then click **Properties** to open the property sheet for the control.
3. Click the **All** tab, and then enter your validation rule in the **Validation Rule** property box.
4. Enter a message in the **Validation Text** property box.

A primary key has several characteristics:

- It uniquely identifies each row.
- It is never empty or null — it always contains a value.
- The values it rarely contains (ideally, never) change.

Set the primary key using fields you already have in Access

For a primary key to work well, the field must uniquely identify each row, never contain an empty or null value, and rarely (ideally, never) change. To set the primary key:

1. Open the database that you want to modify.
2. In the Navigation Pane, right-click the table in which you want to set the primary key and, on the shortcut menu, click **Design View**.
3. Select the field or fields that you want to use as the primary key.To select one field, click the row selector for the field you want.
4.
5. On the **Design** tab, in the **Tools** group, click **Primary Key**.

Remove a primary key in Access

-Removing the primary key does not delete the fields from your table, but it does remove the index that was created for the primary key.

1. Before you can remove a primary key, you must make sure that it does not participate in any table relationships. If you try to remove a primary key that is part of one or more relationships, Access warns you that you must delete the relationships first.

   To delete a table relationship, complete the following steps:

   a. If the tables that participate in the table relationship are open, close them. You cannot delete a table relationship between open tables.
   b. On the **Database Tools** tab, in the **Relationships** group, click **Relationships**.

   c. If the tables that participate in the table relationship are not visible, on the **Design** tab, in the **Relationships** group, click **Show Table**.
   d. Select the tables to add in the **Show Table** dialog box, and then click **Add**, and click **Close**.

e. Click the table relationship line for the table relationship that you want to delete (the line becomes bold when it is selected), and then press the DELETE key.

f. On the **Design** tab, in the **Relationships** group, click **Close**.

2. After you delete the relationships, in the Navigation Pane, right-click the table from which you want to remove the primary key and then click **Design View**.

3. Click the row selector for the current primary key.

4. On the **Design** tab, in the **Tools** group, click **Primary Key**.

What is an index?

-You can use an index to help Access find and sort records faster. An index stores the location of records based on the field or fields that you choose to index. After Access obtains the location from the index, it can then retrieve the data by moving directly to the correct location. In this way, using an index can be considerably faster than scanning through all of the records to find the data.

Multiple-field indexes

You can create an index for that combination of fields,include up to 10 fields in a multiple-field index.

Create an index

To create an index, you first decide whether you want to create a single-field index or a multiple-field index. You create an index on a single field by setting the **Indexed** property.

Create a single-field index

1. In the Navigation Pane, right-click the name of the table that you want to create the index in, and then click **Design View** on the shortcut menu.
2. Click the **Field Name** for the field that you want to index.
3. Under **Field Properties**, click the **General** tab.
4. In the **Indexed** property, click **Yes (Duplicates OK)** if you want to allow duplicates, or **Yes (No Duplicates)** to create a unique index.
5. To save your changes, click **Save** on the **Quick Access Toolbar**, or press CTRL+S.

6.

Create a multiple-field index

1. In the Navigation Pane, right-click the name of the table that you want to create the index in, and then click **Design View** on the shortcut menu.
2. On the **Design** tab, in the **Show/Hide** group, click **Indexes**.

3.

4.

The Indexes window appears. Resize the window so that some blank rows appear and the index properties are shown.

5. In the **Index Name** column, in the first blank row, type a name for the index. You can name the index after one of the index fields, or use another name.
6. In the **Field Name** column, click the arrow and then click the first field that you want to use for the index.
7. In the next row, leave the **Index Name** column blank, and then, in the **Field Name** column, click the second field for the index. Repeat this step until you select all the fields that you want to include in the index.

8.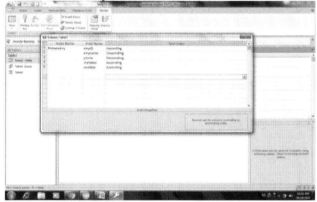
9. To change the sort order of the field's values, in the **Sort Order** column of the Indexes window, click **Ascending** or **Descending**. The default sort order is ascending.
10. In the **Indexes** window, under **Index Properties**, set the index properties for the row in the **Index Name** column that contains the name of the index. Set the features according to the following table.

11. To save your changes, click **Save** on the **Quick Access Toolbar** or press CTRL + S.
12. Close the Indexes window.

Delete an index

1. In the Navigation Pane, right-click the name of the table that you want to delete the index in, and then click **Design View** on the shortcut menu.
2. On the **Design** tab, in the **Show/Hide** group, click **Indexes**.
3. In the Indexes window, select the row or rows that contain the index that you want to delete, and then press DELETE.
4. To save your changes, click **Save** on the **Quick Access Toolbar** or press CTRL + S.
5. Close the **Indexes** window.

Relationships

After you have created a table for each subject in your database, you have to give Access a way to bring that information back together again when needed. You do this by placing common fields in tables that are related, and by defining relationships between your tables.

Types of table relationships

There are three types of table relationships in Access.

1) A one-to-many relationship

To represent a one-to-many relationship in your database design, take the primary key on the "one" side of the relationship and add it as an additional field or fields to the table on the "many" side of the relationship.

2) A many-to-many relationship

To represent a many-to-many relationship, you must create a third table, often called a junction table, that breaks down the many-to-many relationship into two one-to-many relationships. You insert the primary key from each of the two tables into the third table. As a result, the third table records each occurrence, for instance, of the relationship

3) A one-to-one relationship

In a one-to-one relationship, each record in the first table can have only one matching record in the second table, and each record in the second table can have only one matching record in the first table. This relationship is not common because, most often, the information related in this way is stored in the same table.

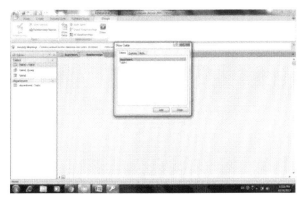

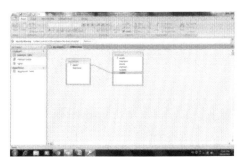

Chapter 2. Table Relationships

Referential integrity

Access rejects any operation that violates referential integrity for that table relationship. This means Access will reject both updates that change the target of a reference and deletions that remove the target of a reference. You need for Access to automatically update all the affected rows as part of a single operation. That way, Access ensures that the update is completed in full so that your database is not left in an inconsistent state, with some rows updated and some not. For this reason, Access supports the **Cascade Update Related Fields** option. When you enforce referential integrity and choose the **Cascade Update Related Fields** option, and you then update a primary key, Access automatically updates all fields that reference the primary key.

For this reason, Access supports the **Cascade Delete Related Records** option. When you enforce referential integrity and choose the **Cascade Delete Related Records** option, and you then delete a record on the primary key side of the relationship, Access automatically deletes all records that reference the primary key.

View table relationships.

Open the Relationships window

1. Click **File**, and then click **Open**.
2. Select and open the database.
3. On the **Database Tools** tab, in the **Relationships** group, click **Relationships**.

   If the database contains relationships, the Relationships window appears. If the database does not contain any relationships and you are opening the Relationships window for the first time, the **Show Table** dialog box appears. Click **Close** to close the dialog box.

4. On the **Design** tab, in the **Relationships** group, click **All Relationships**.

   This displays all of the defined relationships in your database. Note that hidden tables (tables for which the **Hidden** checkbox in the table's **Properties** dialog box is selected) and their relationships will not be shown unless the **Show Hidden Objects** check box is selected in the **Navigation Options** dialog box.

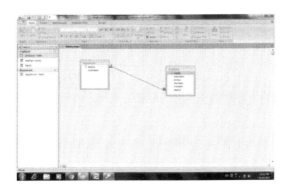

When the Relationships window is active, you can choose from the following commands on the ribbon:

On the **Design** tab, in the **Tools** group:

- **Edit Relationships.** Opens the **Edit Relationships** dialog box. When you select a relationship line, you can click **Edit**

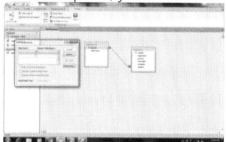

- **Relationships.** To change the table relationship. You can also double-click the relationship line.
- **Clear Layout.** Removes all tables and relationships from display in the Relationships window. Note that this command only hides the tables and relationships — it does not delete them.
- **Relationships Report.** Creates a report that displays the tables and relationships in your database. The report shows only the tables and relationships that are not hidden in the Relationships window.

-

On the **Design** tab, in the **Relationships** group:

- **Show Table.** Opens the **Show Table** dialog box so that you can select tables and queries for viewing in the Relationships window.
- **Hide Table.** Hides the selected table in the Relationships window.
- **Direct Relationships.** Displays all relationships and related tables for the selected table in the Relationships window, if they are not already displayed.
- **All Relationships.** Displays all of the relationships and related tables in your database in the Relationships window. Note that hidden tables (tables for which the **Hidden** checkbox in the table's **Properties** dialog box is selected) and their relationships will not be shown unless Show Hidden Objects is selected in the Navigation Options dialog box.
- **Close.** Closes the Relationships window. If you made any changes to the layout of the Relationships window, you are asked whether to save those changes.

CREATE A TABLE RELATIONSHIP BY USING THE RELATIONSHIPS WINDOW

1. Click **File**, and then click **Open**.
2. Select and open the database.
3. On the **Database Tools** tab, in the **Relationships** group, click **Relationships**.
4. If you have not yet defined any relationships, the **Show Table** dialog box automatically appears. If it does not appear, on the **Design** tab, in the **Relationships** group, click **Show Table**.

   The **Show Table** dialog box displays all of the tables and queries in the database. To see only tables, click **Tables**. To see justqueries, click **Queries**. To see both tables and queries, click **Both**.

5. Select one or more tables or queries and then click **Add**. When you have finished adding tables and queries to the Relationships window, click **Close**.
6. Drag a field (typically the primary key) from one table to the standardfield (the foreign key) in the other table. To drag multiple fields, press the CTRL key, click each field, and then drag them.

   The **Edit Relationships** dialog box appears.

7. Verify that the field names shown are the standard fields for the relationship. If a field name is incorrect, click the field name and select a new field from the list.

8. Click **Create**.

Delete a table relationship

1. On the **Database Tools** tab, in the **Relationships** group, click **Relationships**.

   The Relationships window appears. If you have not yet defined any relationships and this is the first time you are opening the Relationships window, the **Show Table** dialog box appears. If the dialog box appears, click **Close**.
2. On the **Design** tab, in the **Relationships** group, click **All Relationships**.

   All tables that have relationships are displayed, showing relationship lines.
3. Click the relationship line for the relationship that you want to delete. The relationship line appears thicker when it is selected.
4. Press the DELETE key.

   –Or–

   Right-click and then click **Delete**.

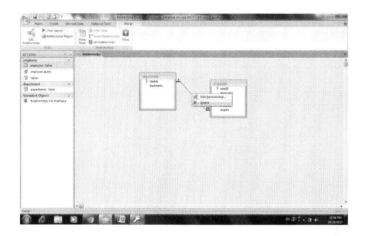

- Access might display the message **Are you sure you want to delete the selected relationship from your database permanently?**. If this confirmation message appears, click **Yes**.

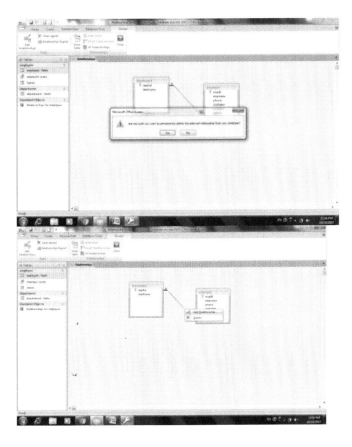

- Make your changes in the Edit Relationships dialog box

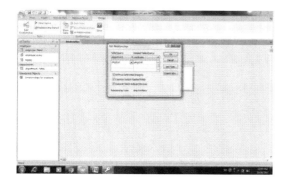

SET THE JOIN TYPE

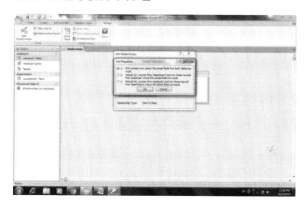

SET THE JOIN TYPE

1. In the **Edit Relationships** dialog box, click **Join Type**.

   The **Join Properties** dialog box appears.

2. Click your choice, and then click **OK**.

IMPORT AND LINK

IMPORT OR LINK TO DATA IN ANOTHER ACCESS DATABASE

You can bring data from one Access database into another in many ways. Copying and pasting is the most straightforward method, but importing and linking offer you better control and flexibility over the data that you bring, and over how you translate that information into the destination database.

Import the data

1. The location of the import wizard differs slightly depending upon your version of Access. Choose the steps that match your Access version:
   - If you are using Access 2007, on the **External Data** tab, in the **Import** group, click **Access**.
2. The **Get External Data - Access Database** import and link wizard opens.

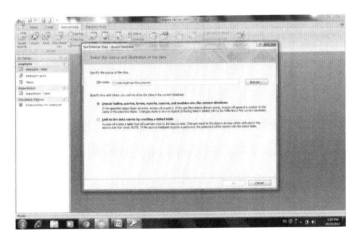

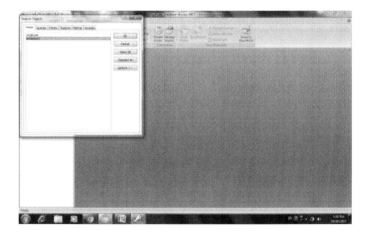

1. In the **File name** text box, type the name of the source database or click **Browse** to display the **File Open**dialog box.
2. Select **Import tables, queries, forms, reports, macros, and modules into the current database** and click **OK**.

   The **Import Objects** dialog box opens.

1. In the **Import Objects** dialog box, on the **Tables** tab, select the tables you want to import. If you 're going to import queries, click the **Queries** tab and select the queries you want to import.

   To cancel a selected object, click the object again.

2. Click **Options** to specify additional settings.

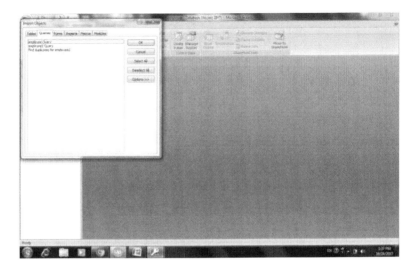

-Click **OK** to finish the operation.

Link to the data

1. The location of the link wizard differs slightly
   depending upon your version of Access. Choose the
   steps that match your Access version:
   o If you are using Access 2007, on the **External
     Data** tab, in the **Import** group, click **Access**.
2. The **Get External Data - Access Database** import and
   link wizard opens
3. In the **File name** text box, type the name of the
   source database or click **Browse** to display the **File
   Open** dialog box.
4. Click **Link to the data source by creating a linked
   table**, and then click **OK**.

   The **Link Tables** dialog box opens.

5. In the **Link Tables** dialog box, select the tables you want to link to.

    To cancel a selection, click the table again.

6. Click **OK** to finish the operation.

    Access creates the linked tables.

7. Open the linked tables in Datasheet view to ensuring that the data looks correct.

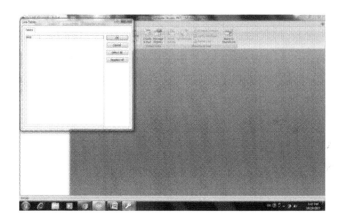

IMPORT A DATABASE OBJECT FROM ANOTHER ACCESS DATABASE INTO YOUR CURRENT DATABASE.

1. Open the database that you want to import objects into if it is not already open. The file format can be either MDB or ACCDB. If the file is in MDE or ACCDE format, you will only be able to import tables and queries from other Access databases. You

cannotimport forms, reports, macros, and modules into an MDE or ACCDE file.

2. The location of the import wizard differs slightly depending upon your version of Access. On the **External Data** tab, in the **Import** group, click **Access**.Access opens the **Get External Data - Access Database** dialog box.

3. In the **File name** text box on the **Get External Data - Access Database** dialog box, type the name of the source database or click **Browse** to display the **File Open** dialog box. Browse to the source database, select it, and then click **Open**.

4. Select **Import tables, queries, forms, reports, macros, and modules into the current database** and click **OK** to open the **Import Objects** dialog box.

5. In the **Import Objects** dialog box, click each tab and select the objects you want. To cancel a selected object, click the object again. To select all objects for import on the current tab, click **Select All**. Click **Deselect All** to cancel picking all objects on the

current tab

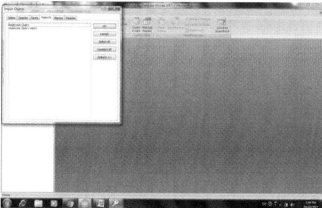

6. Click **Options** to specify additional settings. The following table describes how each option impacts the results of the operation.

7. Click **OK** to start the import operation.

IMPORT OR LINK TO DATA IN AN EXCEL WORKBOOK

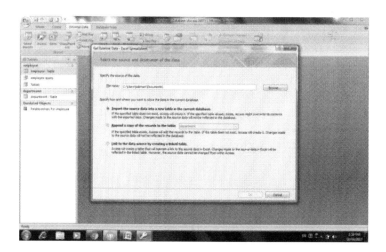

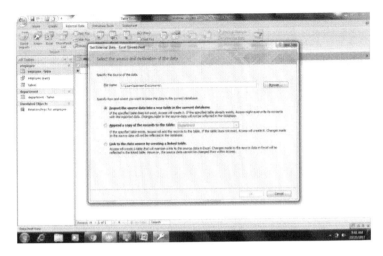

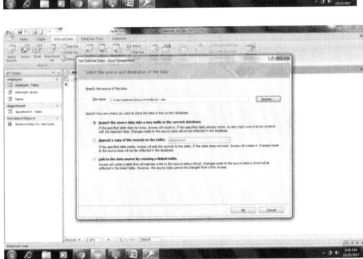

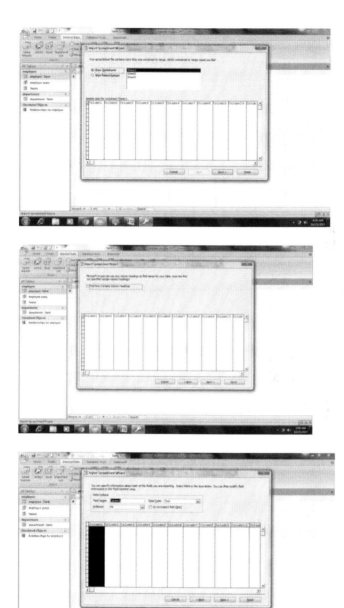

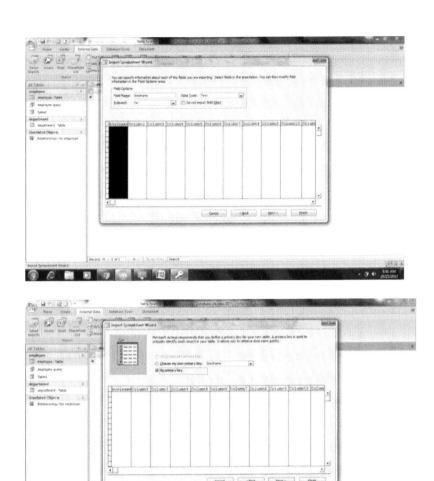

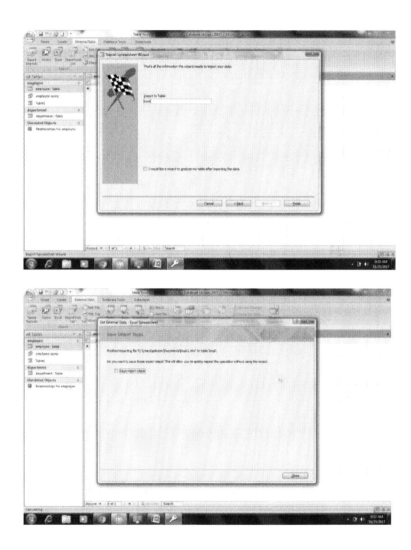

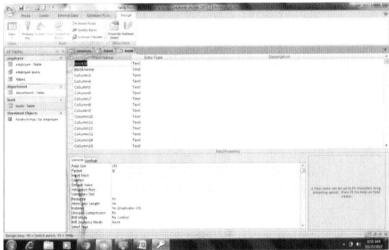

USE THE IMPORT SPREADSHEET WIZARD

1. On the first page of the wizard, select the worksheet that contains the data that you want to import, and then click **Next**.
2. On the second page of the wizard, click either **Show Worksheets** or **Show Named Ranges**, select either

the worksheet or the named range that you want to import, and then click **Next**.

3. If the first row of the source worksheet or range contains the field names, select **First Row Contains Column Headings** and click **Next**.

    To create an index on the field set **Indexed** to **Yes**.

    o   To entirely skip a source column, select the **Do not import field (Skip)** check box.

    Click **Next** after you finish selecting options.

4. In the next screen, specify a primary key for the table. If you select **Let Access add primary key**, Access adds an AutoNumber field as the first field in the destination table, and automatically populates it with unique ID values, starting with 1. Click **Next**.

5. In the final wizard screen, specify a name for the destination table. In the **Import to Table** box, type a name for the table. If the table already exists, Access displays a prompt that asks whether you want to overwrite the existing contents of the table. Click **Yes** to continue or **No** to specify a different name for the destination table, and then click **Finish** to import the data.

6. Click **Yes** to save the details of the operation for future use. Keeping the details helps you repeat the operation at a later time without having to step through the wizard each time.

Import SQL Server data

Importing SQL Server data creates a copy of the data in an Access database. During the import operation, you specify the tables or views that you want to copy.

The import operation creates a table in Access and then copies the data from the SQL Server database into the Access table.

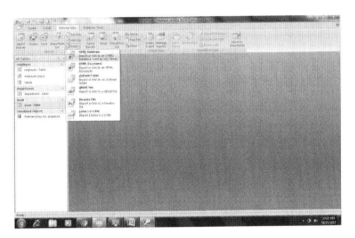

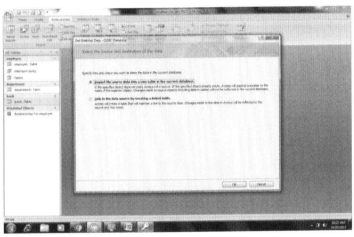

Import the data

1. Open the destination database.

   On the **External Data** tab, in the **Import** group, click **More**.

2. Click **ODBC Database**.
3. Click **Import the source data into a new table in the current database**, and then click **OK**.
4. In the **Select Data Source** dialog box, if the .dsn file that you want to use already exists, click the file in the list.

I need to create a new .dsn file

a. Click **New** to create a new data source name (DSN). The Create New Data Source Wizard starts.
b. In the wizard, select **SQL Server** in the list of drivers, and then click **Next**.

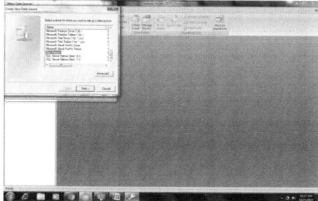

c.
d. Type a name for the .dsn file, or click **Browse** to save the file to a different location.

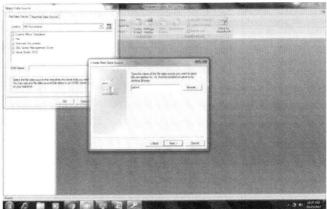

e.

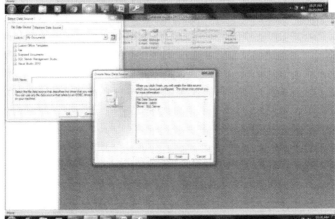

f.

g. Click **Next**, review the summary information and then click **Finish** to complete the wizard.

The Create a New Data Source to SQL Server Wizard starts.

h. In the wizard, type a description of the data source in the **Description** box. This step is optional.

i. Under **Which SQL Server do you want to connect to**, in the **Server** box, type or select the name of the SQL Server to which you want to connect, and then click **Next** to continue.

j. On this page of the wizard, you might need to get information from the SQL Server database administrator, such as determining whether to use Microsoft Windows NT authentication or SQL Server authentication. Click **Next** to continue.

k. On the next page of the wizard, you might need to get more information from the SQL Server database administrator before proceeding. If you want to connect to a specific database, ensure that the **Change the default database to** check box is selected. Then select the database that you want to work with, and then click **Next**.

l. Click **Finish**. Review the summary information, and then click **Test Data Source**.

m. Review the test results, and then click **OK** to close the **SQL Server ODBC Data Source Test** dialog box.

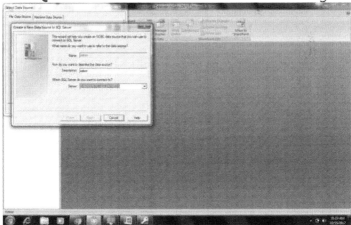

n.

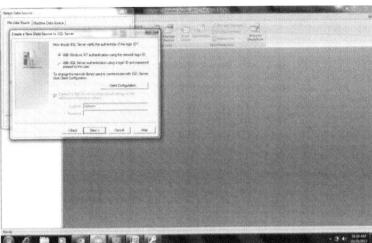

O.

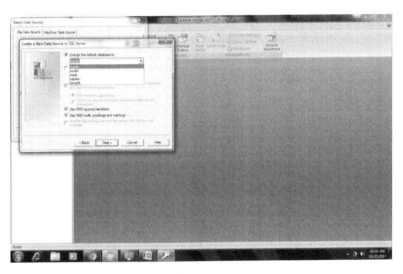

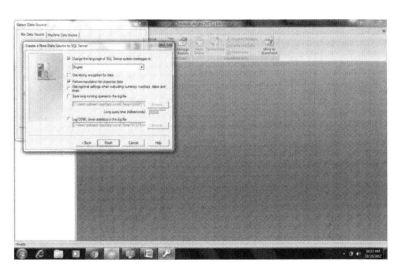

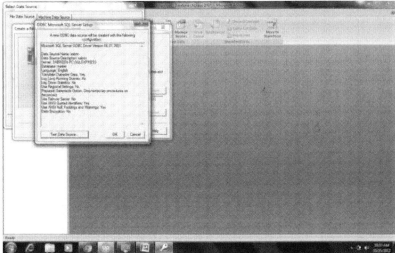

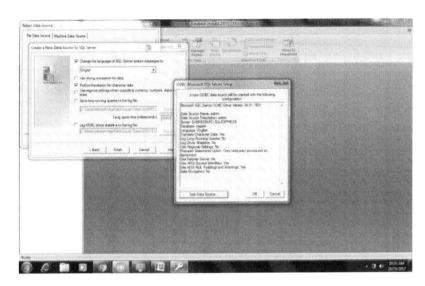

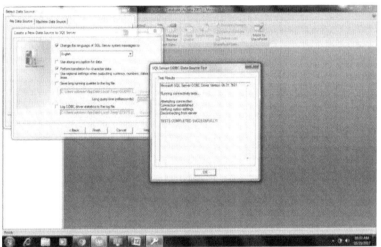

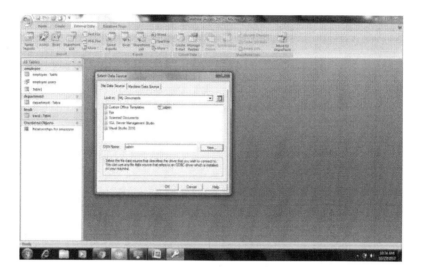

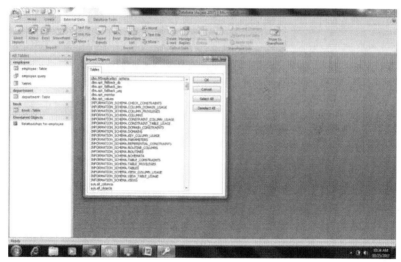

If the test was successful, click **OK** again to complete the wizard, or click **Cancel** to return to the wizard and make changes to your settings.

5. Click **OK** to close the **Select Data Source** dialog box.

Access displays the **Import Objects** dialog box.

6. Under **Tables**, click each table or view that you want to import, and then click **OK**.
7. If the **Select Unique Record Identifier** dialog box appears, Access was unable to determine which field or fields uniquely identify each row of a particular object. In this case, select the field or combination of fields that is unique for each row, and then click **OK**. Click **Close** under **Save Import Steps** in the **Get External Data - ODBC Database** dialog box. Access completes the import operation and displays the new table or tables in the Navigation Pane.

Save the import steps as a specification

1. Under **Save Import Steps** in the **Get External Data - ODBC Database** dialog box, select the **Save import steps** check box.

   A set of additional controls appears.

2. In the **Save as** a box, type a name for the import specification.
3. Type a description in the **Description** box. This step is optional.
4. If you want to operate at fixed intervals (such as weekly or monthly), select the **Create Outlook Task** check box. This creates a task in Microsoft Office Outlook 2007 that lets you run the specification.
5. Click **Save Import**.

Configure the Outlook task

If you selected the **Create Outlook Task** check box in the previous procedure, Access starts Office Outlook 2007 and displays a new task. Follow these steps to configure the task

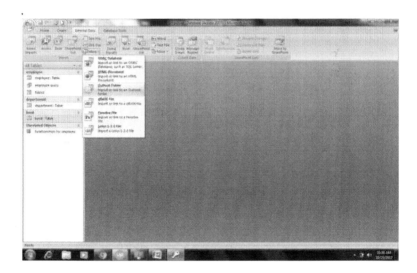

1. In the Outlook task window, review and modify the task settings, such as **Due date** and **Reminder**.

    To make the task recur, click **Recurrence** and fill in the appropriate information.

2. When you finish with the task settings in Outlook, on the **Task** tab, in the **Actions** group, click **Save and Close**.

Run a saved task

1. In the Outlook Navigation Pane, click **Tasks**, and then double-click the task that you want to run.
2. On the **Task** tab, in the **Microsoft Office Access** group, click **Run Import**.
3. Switch back to the Access window, and then press F5 to refresh the Navigation Pane.
4. Double-click the imported table to open it in Datasheet view.
5. Ensure that all of the fields and records were imported and that there are no errors.
6. Right-click the imported table in the Navigation Pane, and then click **Design View** on the shortcut menu. Review the field data types and other field properties.

Link to SQL Server data

Linking lets, you connect to data without importing that information, so that you can view and edit the latest data both in the SQL Server database and in your Access database without creating and maintaining a copy of the data in Access. If you do not want to copy SQL Server data into your Access database, but instead you want to run queries and generate reports that are based on that data, you should link rather than import.

Steps to Link to the data is the same steps for importing data

Access displays the **Link Tables** dialog box.

1. Under **Tables**, click each table or view that you want to link to, and then click **OK**.
2. If the **Select Unique Record Identifier** dialog box appears, Access was unable to determine which field or fields uniquely identify each row of the source data. In this case, select the field or combination of fields that is unique for each row, and then click **OK**. If you are not sure, check with the SQL Server database administrator.

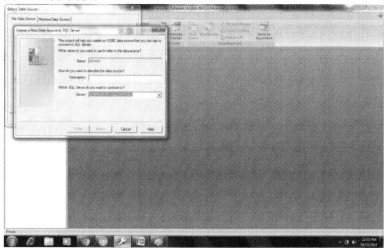

3.

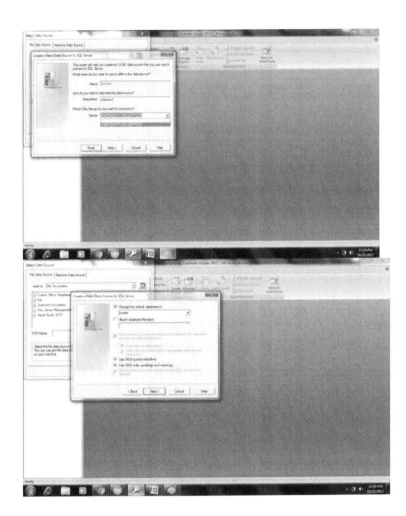

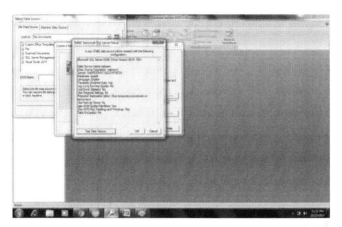

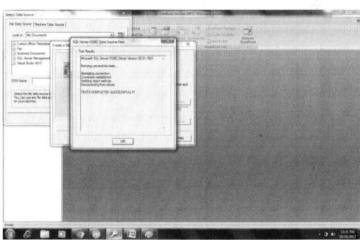

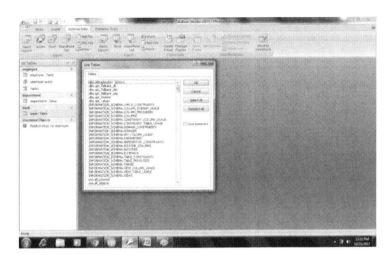

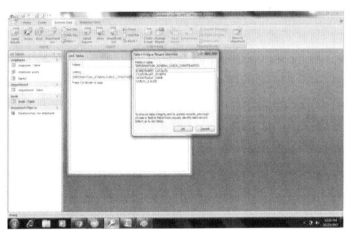

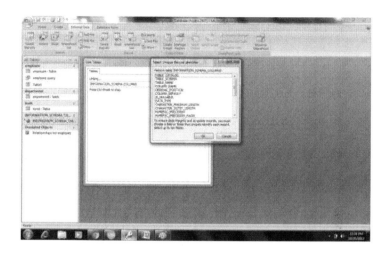

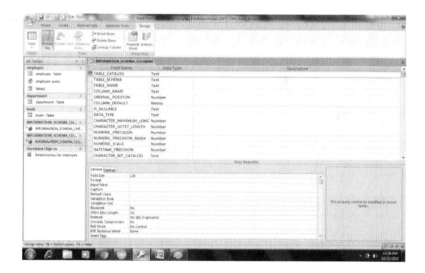

Access completes the linking operation and displays the new linked table or tables in the Navigation Pane.

To update a linked table by applying the latest SQL Server object structure:

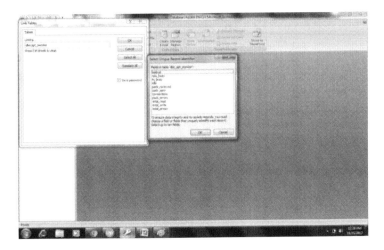

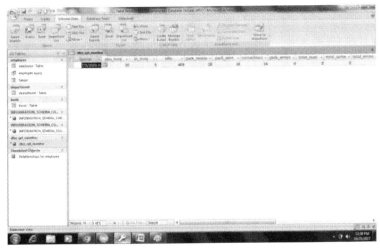

1. Right-click the table in the Navigation Pane, and then click **Linked Table Manager** on the shortcut menu.
2. Select the checkbox next to each linked table that you want to update, or click **Select All** to select all of the linked tables.
3. Click **OK**.
4. Click **Close** to close the Linked Table Manager.

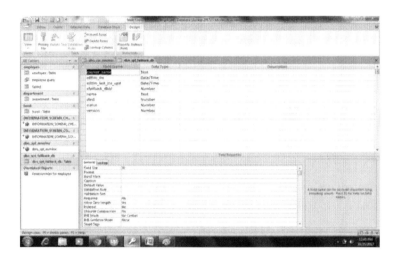

IMPORT OR LINK TO DATA IN A TEXT FILE

You can bring data from a text file into Access in two ways. If you want a copy of the data that you can edit within Access, import the file into a new or existing table by using the Import Text Wizard. If you merely want to view the latest source data within Access for more affluent querying and reporting, create a link to the text file in your database by using the Link Text Wizard.

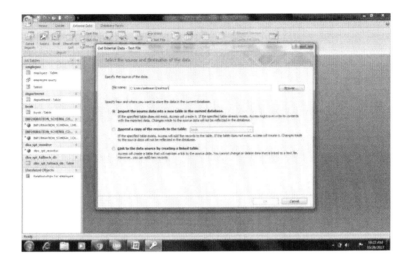

1. Close the source file, if it is open. Keeping the source file open might result in data conversion errors during the import operation.

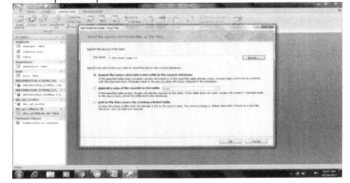

2.

1. The location of the import/link text wizard differs slightly depending upon your version of Access.
   o If you're using Access 2007, on the **External Data** tab, in the **Import** group, click **Text File**.

2. Access opens the **Get External Data – Text File** dialog box.
3. In the **Get External Data - Text File** dialog box, in the **File name** box, type the name of the source file.
4. Specify how you want to store the imported data.
   o To store the data in a new table, select **Import the source data into a new table in the current database**. You will be prompted to name this table later.
   o To append the data to an existing table, select **Append a copy of the records to the table** and then select a table from the drop-down list.
5. Click **OK**.
6. If you chose to append the data, skip to step 13. If you are importing the data into a new table, click **Next**. At this point, you should review the field properties displayed in the wizard.
7.

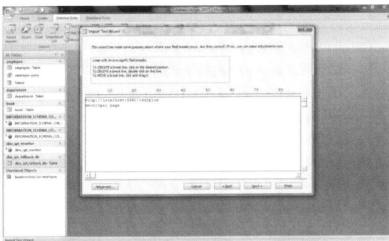

8.

9.

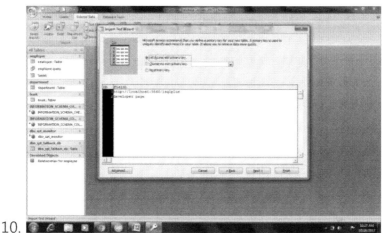

10.

11. Click a column in the lower half of the wizard page to display the corresponding field's properties. Review and change, if you want, the name and data type of the destination field.

   -To create an index on the field set **Indexed** to **Yes**. To altogether skip a source column, select the **Do not import field (Skip)** check box. Then click **Next**.

12. Access displays the final page of the wizard. If you are importing records into a new table, specify a name for the destination table. In the **Import to Table** box, type a name for the table. If the table already exists, a prompt asks you whether you want to overwrite the existing contents of the table. Click **Yes** to continue or **No** to specify a different name for the destination table.

13.

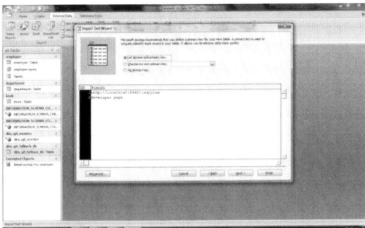

14.

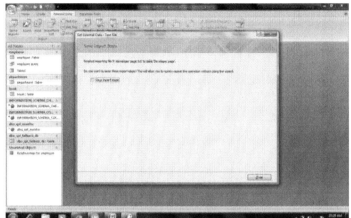

15.

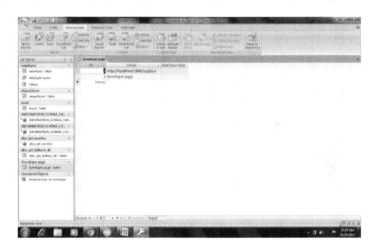

16. Click **Finish** to import the data.
17. Open the destination table in Datasheet view.
    Compare the data in the table with the source file, and
    make sure the data appears to be correct.

Link to a text file

- When you link to a text file, Access creates a new
  table, often referred to as a linked table. The linked

table shows the data from the source file, but it doesn't store the data in the database.

- You cannot link a text file to an existing table in the database. In other words, you cannot append data to a current table by performing a linking operation.
- A database can contain multiple linked tables.
- Any changes that you make to the source file are automatically reflected in the linked table. However, the contents and structure of a linked table in Access are read-only.
- When you open a text file in Access, Access creates a blank database and automatically starts the Link Text Wizard.

STEPS FOR LINKING TO A TEXT FILE

1. Locate the text file, and open it in a word processing program, such as Word or Notepad.
2. Review the contents of the source file, and take action
3. Close the source file, if it is open.
4. Open the database in which you want to create the link. Ensure that the database is not read-only and that you have the necessary permissions to make changes to the database.
   - The location of the import/link text wizard differs slightly depending upon your version of Access.
   - If you are using Access 2007, on the **External Data** tab, in the **Import** group, click **Text File**.
5. Access opens the **Get External Data – Text File** dialog box.

6. In the **Get External Data - Text File** dialog box, specify the name of the text file that contains the data to which you want to link in the **File name** box.
7. Select **Link to the data source by creating a linked table** and then click **OK**.
8. Access scans the contents of the file and suggests how the file is organized. If the file uses a delimiting character to separate the fields, you should ensure that the **Delimited** option is selected. If the file has fixed-width fields, ensure that the **Fixed Width** option is selected.
9. Click **Next**.
10. The next page of the wizard that is displayed depends on whether you selected the delimited option or the fixed-width option, then, click **Next**.
11. On the next page of the wizard, Access displays the field properties. Click a column in the lower half of the wizard page to display the corresponding field's properties. Review and change, if you want, the name and data type of the destination fields.
12. Click **Next**.
13. On the final page of the wizard, specify a name for the linked table and click **Finish**. If a table with that name already exists, Access asks if you want to overwrite the existing table. Click **Yes** if you're going to overwrite, or **No** to specify a different table name.

Access attempts to create the linked table. If the table is successfully created, Access displays the message **Finished linking table...** Open the linked table and review the fields and data to make sure you see the correct data in all the fields.

IMPORT OR LINK TO DATA IN A SHAREPOINT LIST

You can bring data from SharePoint into Access in either of two ways — by importing, or by linking.

The import process creates a copy of the SharePoint list in an Access database. During the import operation, you can specify the records that you want to copy, and, for each selected list, you can specify whether you want to import the entire list or only a specific view.

Complete these steps before you import the list

1. Locate the SharePoint site that contains the lists that you want to copy, and make a note of the site address.

   A valid site address starts with **http://** or **https://** followed by the name of the server, and ends with the path to the specific site on the server.

2. Identify the lists that you want to copy to the database, and then decide whether you want the entire list or just a particular view. You can import multiple lists in a single import operation, but you can import only one view of each list. If necessary, create a

view that contains just the columns and items that interest you.

3. Review the columns in the source list or view.
4. Identify the database into which you want to import the lists.
5. Review the tables in the database.

Import the list

1. Open the Access database in which the imported data will be stored. If you do not want to store the data in any of your existing databases, create a blank database.
2. The location of the import/link text wizard differs slightly depending upon your version of Access.
   - If you are using Access 2007, on the **External Data** tab, in the **Import** group, click **SharePoint List**.
3. Access opens the **Get External Data – SharePoint Site** dialog box.
4. In the wizard, specify the address of the source site.
5. Select the **Import the source data into a new table in the current database** option, and click **Next**.
6. From the list that the wizard displays, select the lists that you want to import.
7. In the **Items to Import** column, select the view that you want for each selected list.
8. The checkboxlabeled **Import display values instead of IDs for fields that look up values stored in another list** controls which data is imported for lookup columns in the selected lists. Do one of the following:

- To import the display values as part of the field itself, select the checkbox. In this case, the field will not look up another table for values.
- For the destination, field to look up another table for values, clear the checkbox. Doing this will copy the IDs of the display value rows to the destination field. The IDs are necessary for defining a lookup field in Access.

When importing IDs, you must import the lists that currently supply the values to the lookup columns (unless the destination database already has tables that could act as lookup tables).

The import operation places the IDs in the corresponding field, but it does not set all of the properties necessary to make the field work as a lookup field,Click **OK**.

LINK TO A SHAREPOINT LIST

When you link to a SharePoint list, Access creates a new table (often referred to as a linked table) that reflects the structure and contents of the source list. Unlike importing, linking establishes a link only to the list, not to any specific views on the list.

- **Import data from a dBASE file**

  dBASE was one of the original database management systems, and the dBASE file format (.dbf) has been around for a long time. Microsoft Access supports importing from and linking to the following dBASE file formats: dBASE III, dBASE IV, dBASE 5, and dBASE 7.

1. Select **External Data**, in the **Import** group select **More**, and then select **dBASE file**.
2. In the **Get External Data – dBASE File** dialog box, select **Browse**.
3. In the **File Open** dialog box, locate the dBASE file, and then click **Open**.
4. In the **Get External Data – dBASE File** dialog box, select **Import the source data into a new table in the current database**, and then select **OK**.
5. Optionally, save the import steps.

LINK TO DATA IN A DBASE FILE

1. Select **External Data**, in the **Import** group select **More**, and then select **dBASE file**.
2. In the **Get External Data – dBASE File** dialog box, select **Browse**.
3. In the **File Open** dialog box, locate the dBASE file, and then click **Open**.
4. In the **Get External Data – dBASE file** dialog box, select **Link to the data source by creating a linked table.**, and then select **OK**.

As a result, a linked table is created with the dBASE data. If there are no column headers in the dBASE file, Access creates default column headers in the linked table.

IMPORT OR LINK TO CONTACTS FROM AN OUTLOOK ADDRESS BOOK

Access and Outlook are both excellent programs for managing your personal and business contacts. As a result, you might want to import or link to contact data from Outlook into Access.

IMPORT OR LINK TO OUTLOOK CONTACTS BY USING THE EXCHANGE/OUTLOOK WIZARD

You can use the **Exchange/Outlook Wizard** to import or link to Outlook contact data. If you import the data, Access creates a copy of the Outlook data and puts it into an Access table. Changes made to the data in either program do not affect the data in the other program. By contrast, if you use the link option, Access maintains a link to the Outlook data. Changes made to the data in Access are reflected in Outlook, and vice versa.

1. The location of the import/link wizard differs slightly depending upon your version of Access. Choose the steps that match your Access version:
2. If you are using Access 2007, on the **External Data** tab, in the **Import** group, click the **More** button to drop down a list of options and then click **Outlook Folder**.
3. In the **Get External Data - Outlook Folder** dialog box, select the option that you want, and then click **OK**.

4. In the **Exchange/Outlook Wizard** dialog box, select the folder or address book that contains the contacts that you want, and then click **Next**.

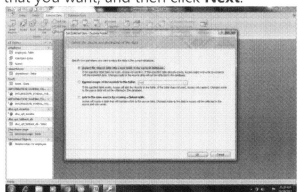

1. Expand the top **Mailbox** folder.

2. Select the folder that contains the contacts that you want to import into Access.

5. Follow the instructions on the remaining pages of the wizard.

IMPORT ACCESS 2.0 AND ACCESS 95 DATABASES INTO CURRENT VERSIONS

If you use an existing database in the Access 2.0 format (.mdb), or the Access 95 format (.mdb) in some cases you can import tables, queries, and macros from that database into a more current version of Access that uses the .accdb file format.

To import forms and reports that contain VBA code (and also modules), first convert your Access 2.0 or Access 95 database to the Access 2002 - 2003 or Access 2000 file format by using Microsoft Office Access 2003, Access 2002, or Access 2000. You can then use a more current version such as Access 2007 to convert that file to the .accdb file format which can then be opened by Access 2010, Access 2013, or Access 2016

OPEN AN ACCESS 2.0 DATABASE IN ACCESS 2007

When you open an Access 2.0 database in Access 2007, Access displays some prompts that, when followed, end with the message **this database was saved in the Microsoft Access 2.0 file format**.

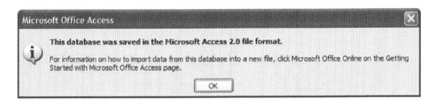

You can import tables, queries, and macros from an Access 2.0 database into an Access 2007 database (.accdb). To import forms, reports, or modules into an Access 2007 database, you first convert the database by using an earlier version of Access, then open the converted database by using Access 2007 and then convert the database into an Access 2007 .accdb file format database.

IMPORT DATA FROM AN ACCESS 2.0 DATABASE INTO ACCESS 2007

1. Open Access 2007, click the **Microsoft Office Button**, and then click **Open**.
2. In the **Open** dialog box, select and open the database that you want to import the tables, queries, or macros into.
3. On the **External Data** tab, in the **Import** group, click **Access**.
4. In the **File name** text box of the Get External Data Wizard, type the name of the source database or click **Browse** to display the **File Open** dialog box and then choose or type the name of the source database.
5. Click **Import tables, queries, forms, reports, macros, and modules into the current database**, and then click **OK**.
6. In the **Import Objects** dialog box, click each tab and select the objects that you want. Remember that you can only import tables, queries, and macros from an Access 2.0 database into Access 2007.

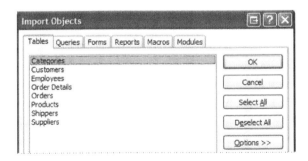

To cancel a selected object, click the object again.

7. Click **Options** to specify additional settings.
8. Click **OK** to finish the operation.

IMPORT DATA FROM AN ACCESS 95 DATABASE INTO ACCESS 2007

To import data from an Access 95 database into Access 2007, you first open the Access 2007 database that you want to import the data into. You then use commands on the **External Data** tab, which involves invoking the Import Wizard.

You can import tables, queries, and macros from an Access 95 format (.mdb) database into an Access 2007 database (.accdb). You can also import forms and reports that do not use VBA code. To import forms and reports that contain VBA code (and also modules), first convert your Access 95 database to the Access 2002 - 2003 or Access 2000 file format by using Microsoft Office Access 2003, Access 2002, or 2000, and then use Access 2007 to convert that file to the Access 2007 .accdb file format.

1. Open Access 2007, click the **Microsoft Office Button**, and then click **Open**.
2. In the **Open** dialog box, select and open the database that you want to import the tables, queries, or macros into.
3. On the **External Data** tab, in the **Import** group, click **Access**.

4. In the **File name** box of the Get External Data Wizard, type the name of the source database or click **Browse** to display the **File Open** dialog box and then choose or type the name of the source database.
5. Click **Import tables, queries, forms, reports, macros, and modules into the current database** and then click **OK**.
6. In the **Import Objects** dialog box, click each tab and select the objects that you want to import.

   To cancel the selection of an object, click the object again.

7. Click **Options** to specify additional settings. These additionalsettings will appear in groups below the list of objects.
8. Click **OK** to finish the operation.

   CONVERT AN ACCESS 2.0 OR ACCESS 95 DATABASE BY USING ACCESS 2003, ACCESS 2002, OR ACCESS 2000

   You can convert an Access 2.0 database to the Access 2000 or Access 2002 - 2003 file format by using one of the versions of Access listed in the following table, provided that you purchase that version of Access and installed it on your computer. Depending on your version of Access, the Access 2.0 converter should already be installed.

   You should convert the Access 2.0 or Access 95 file to the Access 2000 or Access 2002 - 2003 .mdb file format. You can then use Access 2007 to convert the resulting file to the Access 2007 .accdb file format. You can then use the database in Access 2007 or open it in Access 2010, Access 2013, or Access 2016. Depending on your older version of Access, take the following steps:

1. Start Access 2003, Access 2002, or Access 2000.
2. On the **File** menu, click **Open**, and then click the file name for the Access 95 database that you want to convert.
3. On the **Tools** menu, click **Database Utilities**, click **Convert Database** and then click **To Access 2000 File Format**.
4. In the **Convert Database Into** dialog box, enter a filename for the new file, and then click **Save**.

   You might see an informational message warning that you will not be able to use the converted database in earlier versions of Access. If this message appears, click **OK**.

   The file is saved in the Access 2000 file format.

5. Start Access 2007.
6. Click the **Microsoft Office Button**, and then click **Open**.
7. In the **Open** dialog box, select and open the converted database.
8. Click the **Microsoft Office Button**, and then click **Convert**.

9. In the **Save As** dialog box, enter a filename for the Access 2007 file, or accept the file name that is provided, and then clicks **Save**.

The file is saved in the Access 2007 .accdb file format.

Export data to Excel

Using the Export Wizard, you can export data from an Access database to in a file format that can be read by Excel.

When you export data to Excel, Access creates a copy of the selected data and then stores the copied data in a file that can be opened in Excel. If you copy data from Access to Excel frequently, you can save the details of an export operation for future use, and even schedule the export operation to run automatically at set intervals.

CHAPTER 3. EXPORT

EXPORTING DATA TO EXCEL

- Access does not include a "Save As" command for the Excel format. To copy data to Excel, you must use the Export feature described in this article, or you can copy Access data to the clipboard and then paste it into an Excel spreadsheet.
- You can export a table, query, form, or report. You can also export selected records in a multiple-record view, such as a datasheet.
- Microsoft Excel includes a command to import data from an Access database. You can use that command instead of the export command in Access; however, the Excel import command only allows you to import tables or queries.
- You cannot export macros or modules to Excel. When you export a form, report, or datasheet that contains sub-forms, sub-reports, or sub-datasheets, only the primary form, report, or datasheet is exported. You must repeat the export operation for each sub-form, sub-report, and sub-datasheet that you want to export to Excel.
- You can only export one database object in a single export operation. However, you can merge multiple worksheets in Excel after you complete the individual export operations.

EXPORT ONLY A PORTION OF THE DATA

If the object is a table, query, or form, and you want to export only a portion of the data, open the object in Datasheet view and select the records you want.

To open a form in Datasheet view:

a. Double-click the form to open it.
b. Right-click the form, and then click **Datasheet View**. If this option is not available:

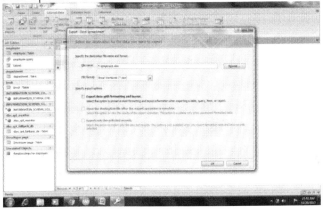

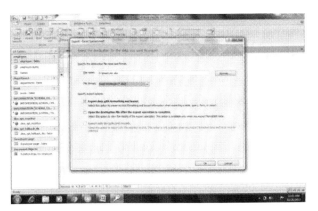

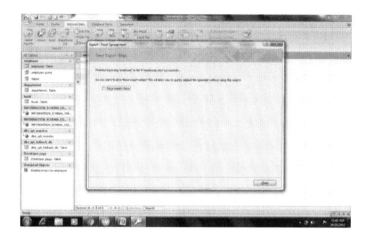

i. Click **Design View**.

ii. Press F4 to display the Property Sheet task pane.

iii. Select **Form** from the drop-down list at the top of the Property Sheet.

iv. On the Format tab of the Property Sheet, set the **Allow Datasheet View** property to **Yes**.

v. On the **Design** tab, in the **Views** group, click **Datasheet View**.

2. On the **External Data** tab, in the **Export** group, click **Excel**.

3. In the **Export - Excel Spreadsheet** dialog box, review the suggested file name for the Excel workbook (Access uses the name of the source object). If you want, you can modify the file name.

4. In the **File Format** box, select the file format that you want.

5. If you are exporting a table or a query, and you want to export formatted data, select **Export data with formatting and layout**

6. To view the destination Excel workbook after the export operation is complete, select the **Open the destination file after the export operation is acomplete** check box.
7. Click **OK**.

EXPORT A DATABASE OBJECT TO ANOTHER ACCESS DATABASE

You can export a table, query, form, report, macro, or module from one Access database to another. When you export an object, Access creates a copy of the object in the destination database.

You export database objects when you need to do any of the following tasks:

- Copy the structure of a table to another database as a shortcut to creating a new table.
- Copy the design and layout of a form or report to another database as a quick way to create a new form or report.
- Copy the latest version of a table or form to another database at regular intervals. To do this, you can create an export specification the first time you export the object, and then use the specification to repeat the operation later.

- You can import multiple objects in a single operation, but you cannot export multiple objects in a single operation. If you want to export multiple objects to another database, it is easier to open the destination database and then perform an import operation from within that database.

- In addition to database objects, you can import relationships between tables, plus any import and export specifications, and menu bars and toolbars. You can also import a query as a table. Exporting does not offer you these options

On the **External Data** tab, in the **Export** group, click **Access**. Note, if you are using Access 2007, click **More** in the **Export** group, and then click **Access Database**.

1. Access opens the **Export - Access Database** dialog box.
2. In the **File name** box on the **Export - Access Database** dialog box, specify the name of the destination database and then click **OK**.
3. In the **Export** dialog box, change the name of the new object if you do not want to overwrite an existing object with the same name in the destination database.
4. If the selected object is a table, specify whether you want to export the table's definition and data, or only the definition.
5. Click **OK** to finish the operation.

EXPORT DATA TO A TEXT FILE

1. In the Access Navigation Pane, right-click the source object, point to **Export** and then click **Text File**. You

can also launch the **Export - Text File** wizard by highlighting the source object in the Navigation Pane and then on the **External Data** tab, in the **Export** group, click **Text File**.

Access opens the **Export - Text File** dialog box.

2. In the **Export - Text File** dialog box, accept or change the name that Access suggests for the text file.
3. If you are exporting a table or a query, and you want to export data with formatting and layout, select the **Export data with formatting and layout** checkbox. If you are exporting a form or a report, the option is always selected but appears dimmed.
4. To view the destination text file after the export operation is complete, select the **Open the destination file after the export operation is acomplete** check box.
5. If the source is a datasheet, and you selected some records in the open datasheet before starting the export operation, you can select the **Export only the selected records** check box. However, if you want to export all of the records that are in the datasheet view, leave the checkbox unselected.
6. Click **OK**.
7. If a text file that you specify in step 2 already exists, Access prompts you to overwrite the file. Click **Yes** to overwrite, or click **No** to return to the **Export - Text File** dialog box to specify a different name.

8. If you are exporting data with formatting and layout, you are asked to choose the encoding to be used for saving the file. Either accept the default, or select the option that you want, and then click **OK**.
9. If you choose to export the data without any formatting or layout, the Export Text Wizard starts and prompts you to select the type of text file that you want to create. Click **Delimited** or **Fixed-Width**, and then click **Next**.
10. Do one of the following sections, based on the choice you made in the previous step:
    o **Delimited**
    ▪ Under **Choose the delimiter that separates your fields**, select or specify the character that delimits the fields - Tab, Semicolon, Comma, Space, or Other.
    ▪ To include the field names in the text file, select the **Include Field Names on First Row** check box.
    ▪ In the **Text Qualifier** list, select the text qualifier (the character that is used to enclose text values). If your source data includes multivalued fields, and if you chose the semicolon as the delimiting character, selecting a text qualifier is very important, because enclosing the value list in a pair of single or double quotation marks helps to keep the values in the value list together.
    o **Fixed-width**
    ▪ Review and position the vertical lines that separate the fields. If necessary, scroll to the right to see all of the fields.

11. On the last page of the wizard, you can edit the file name and path for the text file, or just leave it as it is and click **Next**.

12. Click **Finish**. Access exports the data and displays the status of the export operation on the final page of the wizard.

USE MAIL MERGE TO SEND ACCESS DATA TO WORD

1. Open the Access database that contains the addresses you want to merge with Word.

2. If the Navigation Pane is not open, press F11 to open it.

3. Select the table or query that contains the addresses. The location of the Word Mail Merge wizard differs slightly depending upon your version of Access. Choose the steps that match your Access version:

   o If you are using Access 2007, on the **External Data** tab, in the **Export** group, click the **More** button to drop down a list of options and then click **Merge it with Microsoft Office Word**.

4. The **Microsoft Word Mail Merge Wizard** dialog box opens.
5. Choose whether you want the wizard to link your address data into an existing Word document, or to start with a new, blank document.
6. Click **OK**.

   Word starts and displays the **Mailings** tab and the Mail Merge pane.

1. Work through the wizard steps by clicking the **Next** and **Previous** links at the bottom of the Mail Merge pane.
2. In Step 3 of the wizard, you will not need to select the recipient list. That was determined when you selected it in Access. However, you might want to fine-tune the list by clicking **Edit recipient list**. In the box that opens, you can remove individual recipients from the merge, apply filters, sort the list, and so on.
3. In Step 4 of the wizard, write the letter (unless you are working with an existing document).
4. Place the cursor in the document where you want the address data to appear, and click **Address block**, **Greeting line**, or **More items** in the Mail Merge pane to insert the Access data into the document. In the boxes that appear, select the format you want, and click **Match Fields** to make sure the fields are matched up correctly.
5. In Step 5 of the wizard, click the Next (>>) and Previous (<<) buttons to preview how the merged data will look when you print the document.

6. In Step 6 of the wizard, click **Print** and select the print options you want.
7. Save and close the Word document.

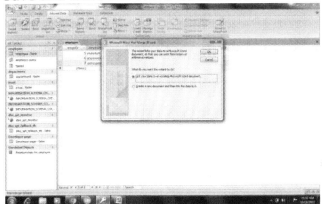

8.

EXPORT ACCESS DATA TO A WORD DOCUMENT

You can export data from your Access database to a Microsoft Word document by using the Export - RTF File Wizard.

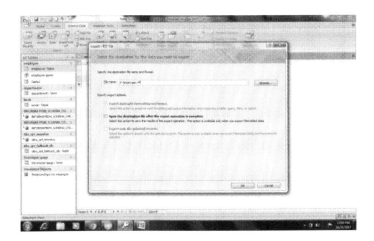

1. The location of the Export - RTF File Wizard differs slightly depending upon your version of Access. Choose the steps that match your Access version:
   - If you are using Access 2007, on the **External Data** tab, in the **Export** group, click **Word**.
2. The **Export - RTF File** export wizard opens.In the **Export - RTF File** wizard, specify the name of the destination file.
3. The wizard always exports formatted data. If you want to view the Word document after the export operation is complete, select the **Open the destination file after the export operation is acomplete**check box.
4. If you selected the records that you want to export before you started the export operation, you couldselect the **Export only the selected records** check box. However, if you want to export all the records in the view, leave the check box cleared.
5. Click **OK**.
6. If the destination document exists, you are prompted to click **Yes** to overwrite the file. Click **No** to change the name of the destination file, and then click **OK** again.

EXPORT A TABLE OR QUERY TO A SHAREPOINT SITE

1. The location of the Export - SharePoint Site Wizard differs slightly depending upon your version of Access. Choose the steps that match your Access version:

o If you are using Access 2007, on the **External Data** tab, in the **Export** group, click **SharePoint List**.

2. The **Export - SharePoint Site** export wizard opens.

3. In the **Specify a SharePoint site** box, enter the address of the destination site.

4. In the **Specify a name for the new list** box, enter a name for the new list.

5. Optionally, enter a description for the new list in the **Description** box, and then select the **Open the list when finished** check box.

6. Click **OK** to start the export process.

7. Access creates a list on the SharePoint site and then displays the status of the operation on the last page of the wizard. When the export operation ends, you can close the wizard or save your export steps as a specification.

CHAPTER 4. FORMS

1) USE THE FORM TOOL TO CREATE A NEW FORM

1. In the Navigation Pane, click the table or query that contains the data you want to see on your form.
2. On the **Create** tab, in the **Forms** group, click **Form**.

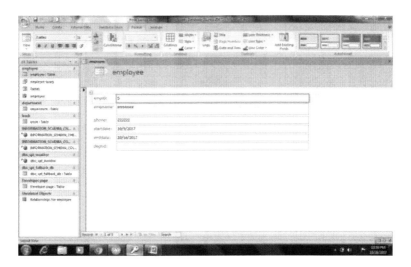

2) CREATE A SPLIT FORM BY USING THE SPLIT FORM TOOL

A split form gives you two views of the data at the same time — a Form view and a Datasheet view.

A split form differs from a form/sub-form combination in that the two views are connected to the same data source and are synchronized with one another at all times. Selecting a field in one part of the form selects the samefield in the other part of the form. You can add, edit, or delete data from either part (as long as the record source is updatable, and you have not configured the form to prevent these actions).

Working with split forms gives you the benefits of both kinds of forms in a single form. For example, you can use the datasheet portion of the formto locate a record quickly, and then use the form portion to view or edit the record.

To create a split form by using the Split Form tool:

1. In the Navigation Pane, click the table or query that contains the data that you want on your form. Alternatively, open the table or query in Datasheet view.
2. On the **Create** tab, in the **Forms** group, click **More Forms**, and then click **Split Form**.

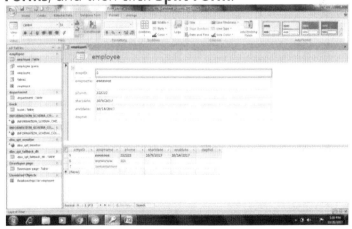

3) CREATE A FORM THAT DISPLAYS MULTIPLE RECORDS BY USING THE MULTIPLE ITEMS TOOL

When you create a form by using the Form tool, the form that Access creates displays a single record at a time. If you want a form that displays multiple records but is more customizable than a datasheet, you can use the Multiple Items tool.

1. In the Navigation Pane, click the table or query that contains the data you want to see on your form.
2. On the **Create** tab, in the **Forms** group, click **More Forms**, and then click **Multiple Items**.

When you use the Multiple Items tool, the form that Access creates resembles a datasheet. The data is arranged in rows and columns, and you see more than one record at a time. However, a Multiple Items form gives you more customization options than a datasheet, such as the ability to add graphical elements, buttons, and other controls.

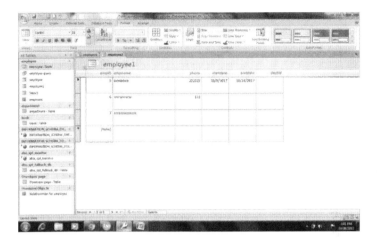

4) CREATE A FORM BY USING THE FORM WIZARD

1. On the **Create** tab, in the **Forms** group, click **Form Wizard**.
2. Follow the directions on the pages of the Form Wizard.
3. On the last page of the wizard, click **Finish**.

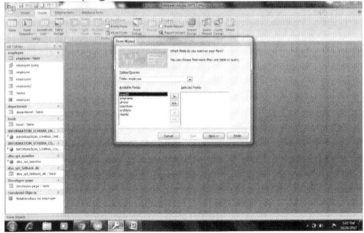

4.

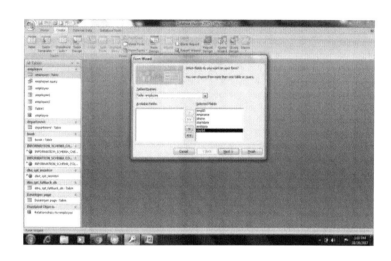

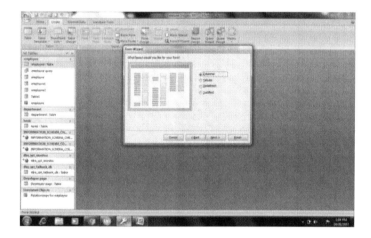

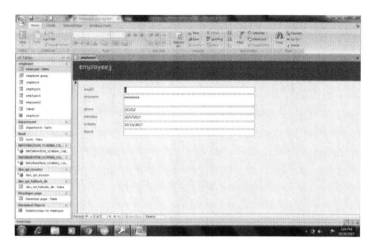

5) CREATE A FORM BY USING THE BLANK FORM TOOL

1. On the **Create** tab, in the **Forms** group, click **Blank Form**.

   Access opens a blank form in Layout view and displays the **Field List** pane.

2. In the **Field List** pane, click the plus sign (+) next to the table or tables that contain the fields that you want to see on the form.
3. To add a field to the form, double-click it or drag it onto the form.
   - After the first field has been added, you can add several fields at once by holding down the CTRL key, clicking several fields, and then dragging them onto the form at the same time.
   - The order of the tables in the **Field List** pane can change, depending on which part of the form is

currently selected. If the field you want to add is not visible, try selecting a different part of the form and then try adding the field again.

4. Use the tools in the **Header/Footer** group on the **Design** tab to add a logo, title, or the date and time of the form.

5. Use the tools in the **Controls** group of the **Design** tab to add a wider variety of controls to the form.

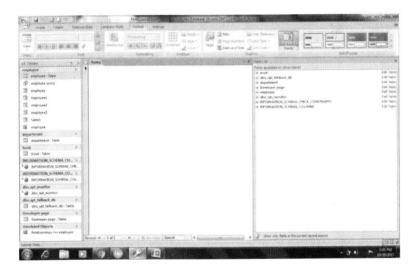

Layout view: to use for form modification, and it can be used for almost all the changes that you would want to make to a form in Access.

Design view   Design view gives you a more detailed view of the structure of your form. You can see the Header, Detail, and Footer sections for the form. The form is not running when it is shown in Design view. Therefore, you cannot see the underlying data while you are making design changes.

You can then drag fields directly from the **Field List** pane onto your form.

- To add a single field, double-click it or drag it from the **Field List** pane to the section on the form where you want it displayed.
- To add several fields at once, hold down CTRL and click the fields that you want to add. Then drag the selected fields onto the form.

  To switch to Design view, right-click the form name in the Navigation Pane and then click **Design View**.

  Access shows the form in Design view.

  You can use the property sheet to change the properties of the form and its controls and sections. To display the property sheet, press F4.

You can use the **Field List** pane to add fields from the underlying table or query to your form design. To display the **Field List** pane:

- On the **Design** tab, in the **Tools** group, click **Add Existing Fields** or use the keyboard shortcut by pressing ALT+F8.

  You can then drag fields directly from the **Field List** pane onto your form.

- To add a single field, double-click it or drag it from the **Field List** pane to the section on the form where you want it displayed.
- To add several fields at once, hold down CTRL and click the fields that you want to add. Then drag the selected fields onto the form.

Create a form from an existing table or query in Access

To create a form from a table or query in your database, in the Navigation Pane, click the table or query that contains the data for your form, and on the **Create** tab, click **Form.**

Create a form that contains a sub-form in Access

When you are working with related data that is stored in separate tables, you often need to view data from multiple tables, or queries in the same form and sub-forms are a convenient way to do this. Since there are

several ways of adding a sub-form depending on your
needs.

Controls

Controls let you view and work with data in your
database application. Controls can be bound,
unbound, or calculated:

- **Bound control.** A control whose source of data is a
  field in a table or query is called a bound control. You
  use bound controls to display values that come from
  fields in your database. The values can be text, dates,
  and numbers, Yes/No values, pictures, or graphs. For
  example, a text box that displays an employee's last
  name might get this information from the Last Name
  field in the Employees table.
- **Unbound control.** A control that doesn't have a
  source of data (such as a field or expression) is called
  an unbound control. You use unbound controls to
  display information, pictures, lines, or rectangles. For
  example, a label that displays the title of a form is an
  unbound control.
- **Calculated control.** A control whose source of data is
  an expression, rather than a field, is called a
  calculatedcontrol. You specify the value that you want
  to use as the source of data in control by defining
  an *expression*. An expression can be a combination of
  operators (such as = and +), control names, field
  names, functions that return a single value, and
  constant values. An expression can use data from a

field in the form or report's underlying table or query, or data from another control on the form or report.

Understand layouts

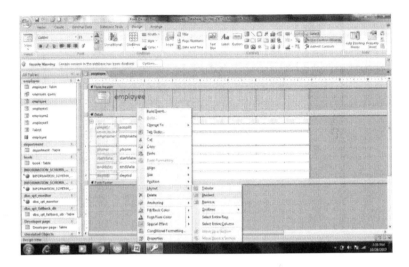

Layouts can be configured in many different ways, but are usually configured in a *tabular* or a *stacked*format. Within these two main formats, you can split or merge cells to customize the layout to suit your controls better.

- In tabular control layouts, controls are arranged in rows and columns like a spreadsheet, with labels across the top,
- Tabular control layouts always span two sections of a form or report.
- In stacked layouts, controls are arranged vertically like you might see on a paper form, with a label to the left of each control,

- Stacked layoutsare always contained within a single section of the form or report.

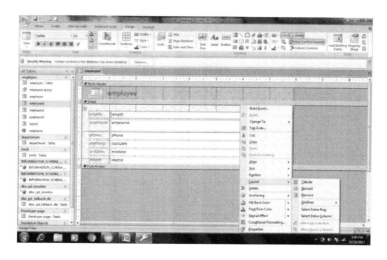

Switch a layout from tabular to stacked, or from stacked to tabular

You can move a control within a layout, or between layouts, by dragging it to the location that you want. As you drag the control, a horizontal or vertical bar indicates where it will be placed when you release the mouse button. If you drag the control over an empty cell, Access highlights the whole cell to indicate where the control will be placed.

You can also move a control within a layout by selecting it, holding down the ALT key, and then use the arrow keys to move the control.

Create a form that contains a sub-form (a one-to-many form)

When you are working with relational data (related data that is stored in separate tables), you often need to view multiple tables or queries on the same form.

A sub-form is a form that is inserted in another form. The primary form is called the mainform, and the form that is enclosed in form is called the sub-form. A form/sub-form combination is sometimes referred to as a hierarchical form, a master/detail form, or a parent/child form.

Sub-forms are especially useful when you want to show data from tables or queries that have a one-to-many relationship.

1. The primary form shows data from the "one" side of the relationship.

2. The sub-form shows data from the "many" side of the relationship.

Create a sub-form by dragging one form onto another

1. Right-click the primaryform in the Navigation Pane, and then click **Design View**.
2. Click the sub-form control one time to select it.
3. If the Property Sheet task pane is not displayed, press F4 to display it.
4. In the Property Sheet, click the **Data** tab.
5. Click the **Build** button next to the **Link Child Fields** property box.

The **Sub-form Field Linker** dialog box appears.

6. In the **Master Fields** and **Child Fields** drop-down lists, select the fields that you want to link the forms with, and then click **OK**. If you are not sure which fields to use, click **Suggest** having Access try to determine the linking fields.
7. Save the main form, switch to Form view, and then verify that the form works as expected.

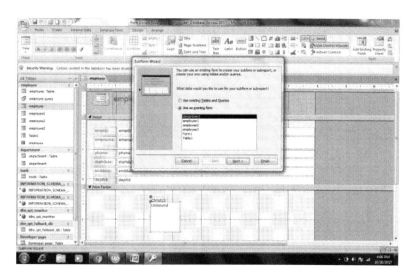

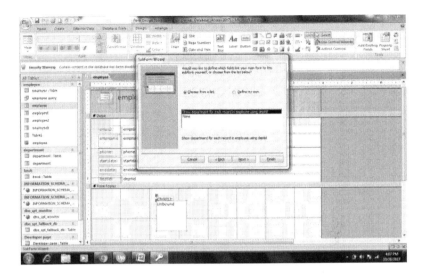

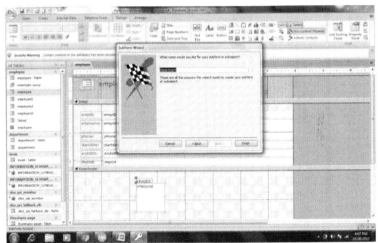

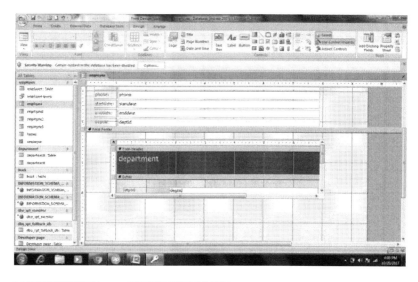

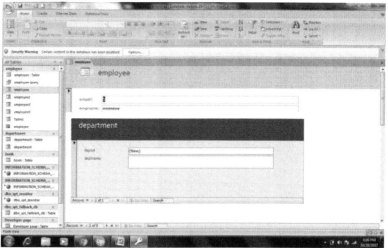

CHANGE THE DEFAULT VIEW OF A SUB-FORM

When you add a sub-form to a form, the sub-
form/sub-report control displays the sub-form
according to the sub-forms **Default View** property.
This property can be set to the following values:

- Single Form
- Continuous Forms
- Datasheet
- Split Form

When you first create a sub-form, this property may be set to **Continuous Forms** or perhaps **Single Form**. However, if you set the **Default View** property of a sub-form to **Datasheet**, then the sub-form will display as a datasheet on the main form.

To set the **Default View** property of a sub-form:

1. Close any open objects.
2. In the Navigation Pane, right-click the sub-form and then click **Design View**.
3. If the Property Sheet is not already displayed, press F4 to display it.
4. In the drop-down list at the top of the Property Sheet, make sure **Form** is selected.
5. On the **Format** tab of the Property Sheet, set the **Default View** property to the view you want to use.
6. Save and close the sub-form, and then open the primary form to check the results.

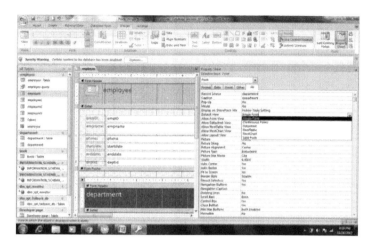

CHANGE THE TAB ORDER FOR CONTROLS

1. In the Navigation Pane, right-click the form and then click **Design View**.
2. On the **Design** tab, in the **Tools** group, click **Tab Order**.
3. In the **Tab Order** dialog box, under **Section**, click the section you want to change.
4. Do one of the following:
   o If you want Access to create a top-to-bottom and left-to-right tab order, click **Auto Order**.
   o If you want to create your custom tab order, click the selector for the control you want to move. (Click and drag to select more than one control at a time.) Click the selector again and drag the control to the desired location in the list.
5. Click **OK**.

REMOVE A CONTROL FROM THE TAB ORDER

1. In the Navigation Pane, right-click the form and then click **Design View**.
2. If the **Property Sheet** task pane is not displayed, press F4 to display it.
3. Select the control that you want to remove from the tab order.
4. On the **Other** tab of the Property Sheet, in the **Tab Stop** property box, click **No**.

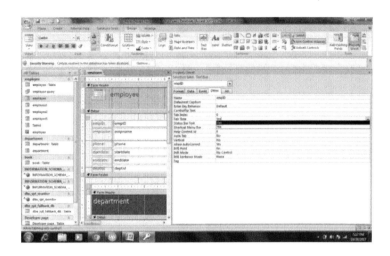

CREATE A LIST OF CHOICES BY USING A LIST BOX OR COMBO BOX

When entering data on forms in Access desktop databases, it can be quicker and easier to select a value from a list than to remember a value to type. A list of choices also helps ensure that the value entered in a field is appropriate. A list control can connect to existing data, or it can display fixed values that you enter when you create the control.

Access provides two list controls for forms — the list box and the combo box.

List box. The list box control displays a list of values or choices. The list box contains rows of data and is usually sized so that several rows are visible at all times. The rows can have one or more columns, which can appear with or without headings. If the list has more rows than can be displayed in control, Access displays a scroll bar in control. The user is limited to the choices given in the list box; it is not possible to type a value into a list box.

Combo box. The combo box control provides a more compact way to present a list of choices; the list is hidden until you click the drop-down arrow. A combo box also gives you the ability to enter a value that is not in the list. In this way, the combo box control combines the features of a text box and a list box.

Create a list box or a combo box by using a wizard

1. Right-click the form in the Navigation Pane, and then click **Design View**.
2. On the **Design** tab, in the **Controls** group, ensure that **Use Control Wizards** is selected.
3. Click either the **List Box** tool or the **Combo Box** tool.

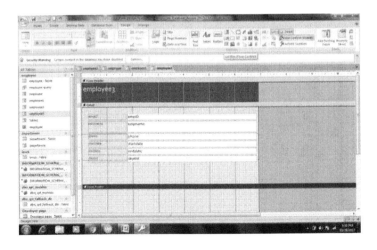

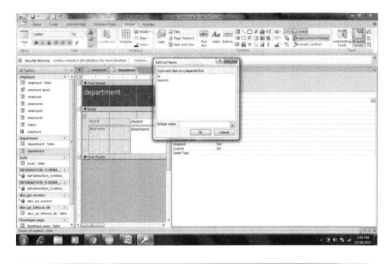

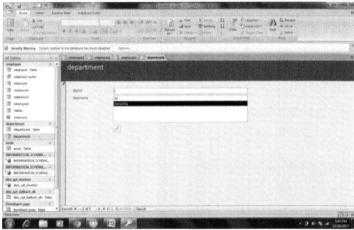

PREVENT THE EDITING OF THE VALUE LIST IN FORM VIEW

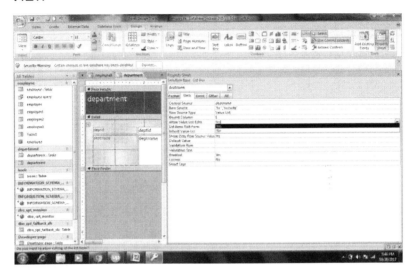

1. Right-click the form in the Navigation Pane and click **Design view** or **Layout view**.
2. Click the control to select it, and then press F4 to display the property sheet.
3. On the **Data** tab of the property sheet, set the **Allow Value List Edits** property to **No**.
4. Click **File** and then click **Save**

- **Change the sort order in a list box or combo box.** If you used a wizard to create the list box or combo box, Access automatically sorts the rows that make up the list by the first visible column. If you want to specify a different sort order, or if you have set the **Row Source** property of the control to a saved query, use the following procedure:

- o Click the **Data** tab, and then click the **Row Source** property box.
- o On the **Data** tab of the property sheet, click to open the Query Builder.
- o In the **Sort** row for the column, you want to sort, specify the sort order you want.
- • **Turn off the fill-in-as-you-type feature for a combo box on a form**
- o In the **Auto Expand** property box, click **No**.

   When the **Auto Expand** property is set to **No**, you must select a value from the list or type the entire value.

SET A DEFAULT VALUE

1. In the Navigation Pane, right-click the table that you want to change, and then click **Design View**.
2. Select the field that you want to change.
3. On the **General** tab, type a value in the **Default Value** property box.

   The value you that you can enter depends on the data type that is set for the field. For example, you can type **=Date()** to insert the current date in a Date/Time field

4. Save your changes.Press CTRL+S to save your changes.

ADD A COMMAND BUTTON TO A FORM BY USING A WIZARD

1. Right-click the form in the Navigation Pane, and then click **Design view** on the shortcut menu.
2. On the **Design** tab, in the **Controls** group, ensure that **Use Control Wizards** is selected.
3. On the **Design** tab, in the **Controls** group, click **Button**.

4. In the design grid, click where you want the command button to be inserted.

   The Command Button Wizard starts.

5. Follow the directions in the wizard. On the last page, click **Finish**.

   The wizard creates the command button and embeds a macro in the buttons **On Click** property. The macro contains actions that perform the task you chose in the wizard.

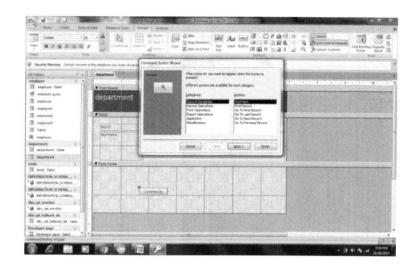

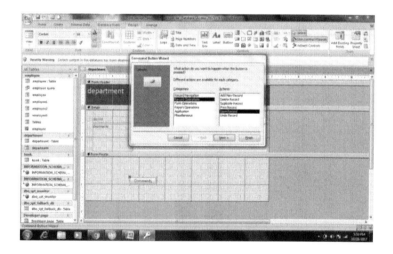

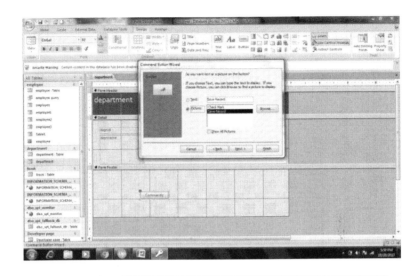

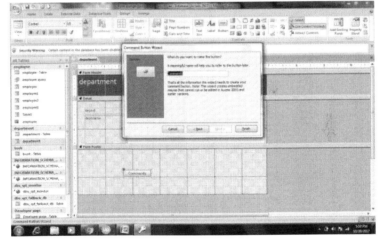

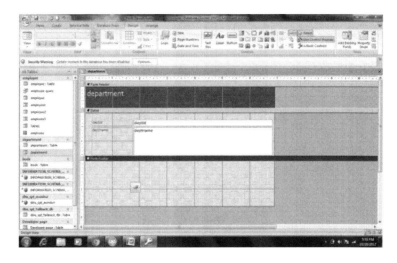

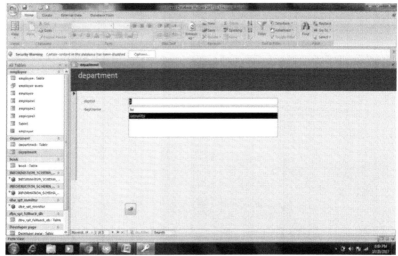

Make a command button appear as a hyperlink

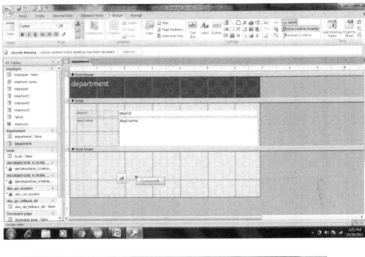

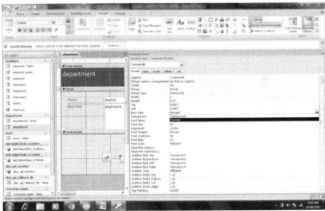

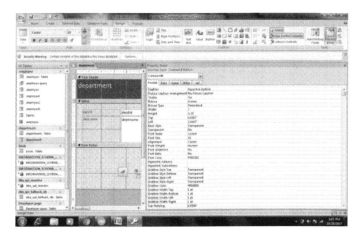

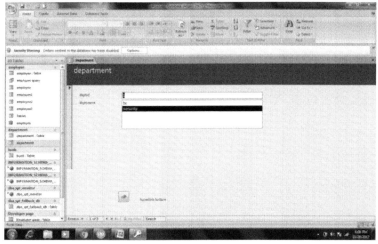

i.   Click the command button to select it and press F4 to display its property sheet.

ii. On the **Format** tab of the property sheet, click in the **Back Style** property box.

iii. In the drop-down list, select **Transparently**.

The body of the command button is hidden, but its caption remains visible.

iv. To underline or change the color of the text in the caption, use the tools in the **Font** group on the **Format** tab.

o **Create a Cancel button**

i. Click the command button, and then press F4 to open its property sheet.

ii. In the **Cancel** property box, click **Yes**.

When a command button's **Cancel** property is set to **Yes**, and the form is the active form, a user can select the command button by clicking it, pressing the ESC key, or pressing ENTER when the command button has focus. When the **Cancel** property is set to **Yes** for any one command button, that property is automatically set to **No** for all other command buttons on the form.

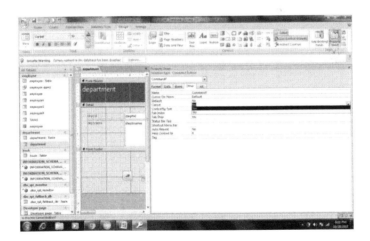

ADD A CHECKBOX CONTROL TO SHOW YES/NO VALUES

In Access, a Yes/No field stores only two values: Yes or No. If you use a text box to display a Yes/No field, the value displays as -1 for Yes and 0 for No. These values are not very meaningful for most users, so Access provides check boxes, option buttons, and toggle buttons that you can use to display and enter Yes/No values. These controls provide a graphic representation of the Yes/No value that is both easy to use and easy to read.

A checkbox is the best control for representing a Yes/No value. This is the default type of control that is created when you add a Yes/No field to a form or report. By contrast, option buttons and toggle buttons are most often used as part of an option group.

Create a bound check box, option button, or toggle button

1. Open the form or report in Layout view or Design view by right-clicking it in the Navigation Pane, and then click the view you want on the shortcut menu.
2. If the **Field List** pane is not already displayed, press ALT+F8 to display it.
3. Expand the table lists, if needed by clicking the plus signs (+) next to the table names.
4. Drag the Yes/No field from the **Field List** pane to the form or report.

Depending on the setting of the field's **Display Control** property, a checkbox, a text box, or a combo box is created and bound to the field. When you create a new Yes/No field in a table, the default setting of the field's **Display Control** property is **CheckBox**.

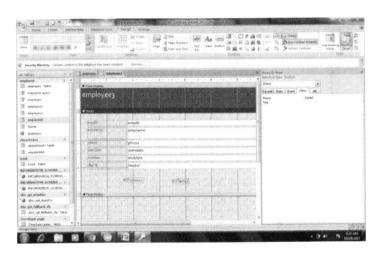

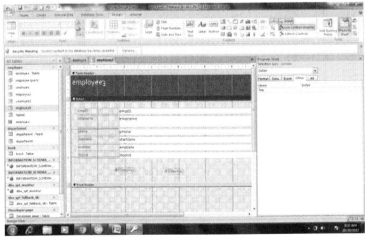

CREATE AN UNBOUND CHECK BOX, OPTION BUTTON, OR TOGGLE BUTTON IS THE SAME METHOD FOR BOUNDED CHECKBOX

RENAME THE CONTROL

1. Ensure that the control is selected.
2. If the property sheet is not already displayed, press F4 to display it.
3. Type a new name in the **Name** property box of the control.

Create an option group

1. Open the form in Design view by right-clicking it in the Navigation Pane, and then clicking **Design View**.
2. On the **Design** tab, in the **Controls** group, ensure that **Use Control Wizards** is selected.
3. In the same group, click **Option Group**.

4. Click on the form where you want to place the option group.
5. Follow the instructions in the wizard. On the last page, click **Finish**.

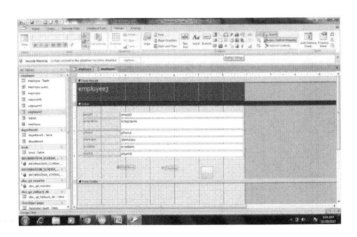

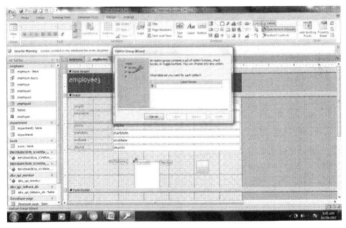

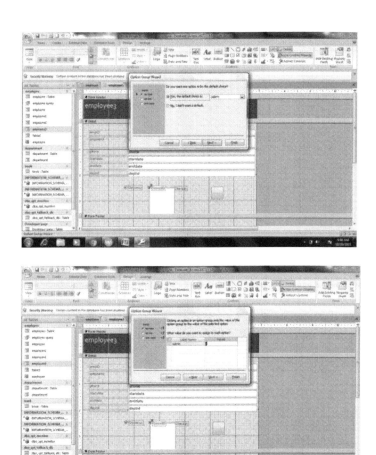

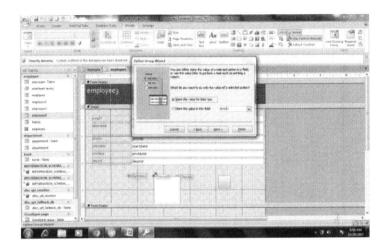

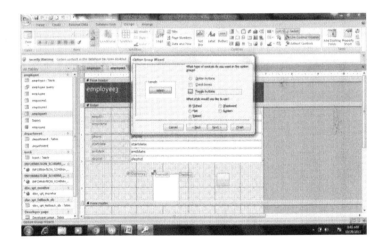

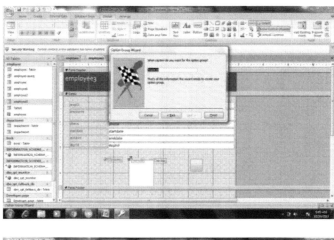

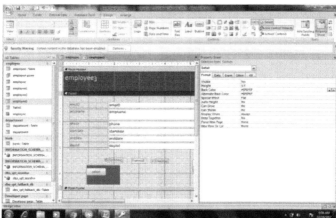

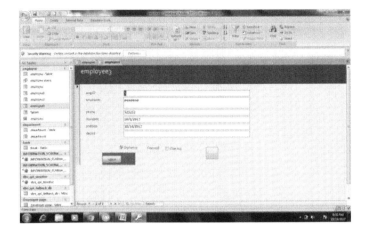

CHAPTER 5. INTRODUCTION TO REPORTS

Reports offer a way to view, format, and summarize the information in your Microsoft Access database. For example, you can create a simple report of phone numbers for all your contacts, or a summary report on the total sales across different regions and time periods.

START THE REPORT WIZARD

1. On the **Create** tab, in the **Reports** group, click **Report Wizard**.

   Access starts the **Report Wizard**.

1. Click the **Tables/Queries** drop-down list and choose the table or query that contains the fields you want on your report.
2. Double-click fields in the **Available Fields** list to choose them.

   Access moves them to the **Selected Fields** list. Alternatively, you can click the buttons located between the **Available Fields** box and the **Selected Fields** box to add or remove the selected field or to add all or remove all of the fields.

3. If there are fields in another table or query that you also want to put on your report, click

the **Tables/Queries** drop-down list again and choose the other table or query, and continue to add fields.

4. After you have finished adding fields, click **Next**.

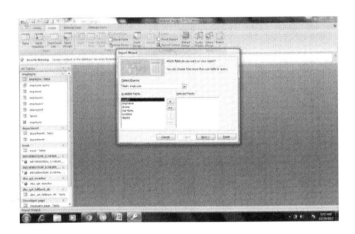

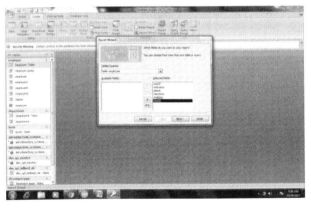

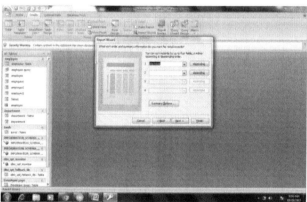

Sort and Summarize Records

You can sort records by up to four fields, in either ascending or descending order.

1. Click the first drop-down list and choose a field on which to sort.

You can click the button to the right of the list to toggle between ascending and descending order

(**Ascending** is the default). Optionally, click the second, third, and fourth drop-down lists to choose additional sort fields.

2. Click Summary Options if you want to summarize any of the numeric fields.

Note that the Summary Options button will only be visible if you have one or more numeric fields in the Detail section your report. The wizard displays the available numeric fields.

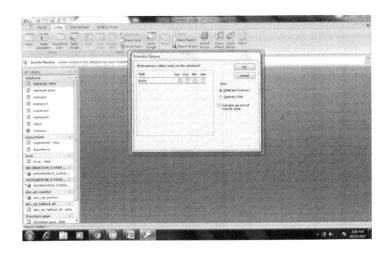

1. Select the checkbox under your choice of **Sum**, **Avg**, **Min** or **Max** to include those calculations in the group footer.

You can also choose to show the details and summary or the summary only. Click **OK**.

2. Follow the directions on the remaining pages of the Report Wizard. On the last page, you can edit the title of the report. This title will be displayed on the first page of the report, and Access will also save the report, using the title as the document name. You can edit both the title and the document name later.
3. Click **Finish**. Access automatically saves the report and displays it in Print Preview, which shows you the report as it will look when printed.

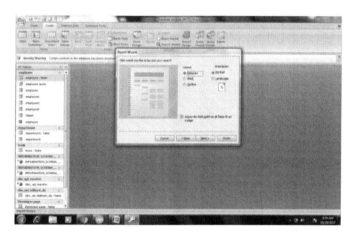

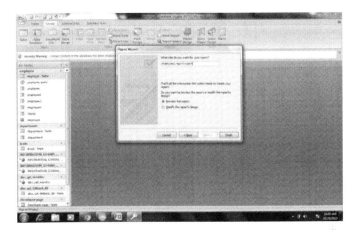

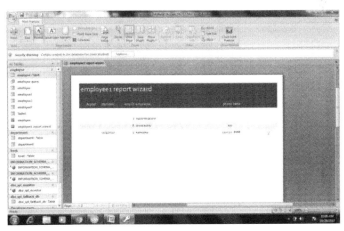

Filter Data in a Report

To filter data in a report, open it in Report view (right-click it in the Navigation pane and click **Report View**). Then, right-click the data you want to filter.

For example, in a report listing all employees, you might want to limit the report to employees whose empname start with "L":

1. Right-click any last name, and click **Text Filters** > **Begins With**.

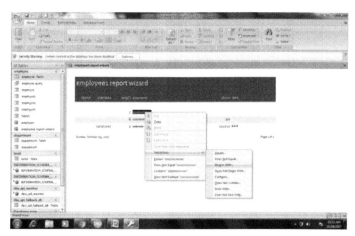

2. Enter "L" in the box that appears, and click **OK**.

Access applies the filter, and now you can print the report with just that data.

3.

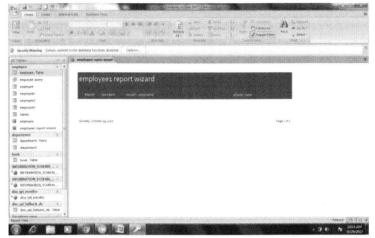

Toggle or clear filters

On the **Home** tab, click the **Toggle Filter** button to remove and reapply the filter as needed.

If you close the report without explicitly clearing the filters, Access remembers them, and you can click **Toggle Filter** again to reapply the next time you open the report. This works even if you close and reopen the database. However, if you click **Home** > **Advanced** > **Clear All Filters**, Access clears the filters entirely and you will need to start from scratch next time around.

Save filters as a query

If you have manyfilters applied to a report, you might want to save the filters as a query. Then you can use the query as the data source for the current report or a new report, or just run the query next time you want to see the data.

1. Apply the filters, and
   click **Home** > **Advanced** > **Advanced Filter/Sort**.

2. Click **Save**, and enter a name for the query.

SET PRINT OPTIONS

SELECT PAGE SETUP OPTIONS

After you create your report, you can set options for the print layout in the **Page Setup** dialog box. These options help you fine tune the format with options for margin settings, use of gridlines and columns, or print only the data from the report without the formatting.

To set the print page options, complete the following steps:

1. In the Navigation Pane, right-click the report and then click **Print Preview**.
2. On the **Print Preview** tab, in the **Page Layout** group, click **Page Setup** and set the margins, orientation and column settings that you want.

3.

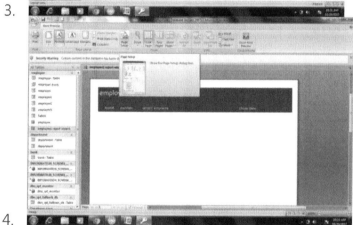

4.

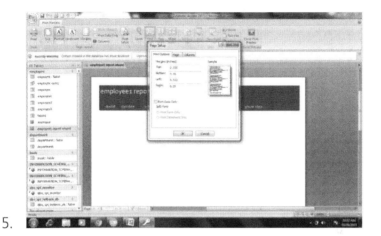

5.

Print Options tab settings

To customize the margins on your report, on the **Print Preview** tab, in the **Page Size** group, click **Margins**and select a suitable option and a preview of the report with the changed margin settings are displayed.

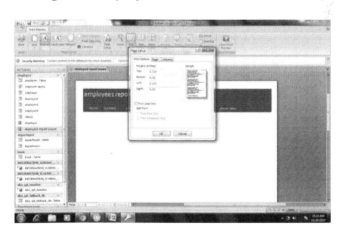

Page tab settings

Columns tab settings

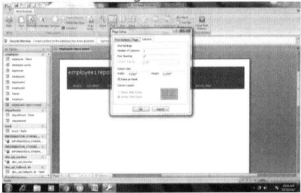

SELECT PRINTER SETTINGS

After you complete the page setup settings for your report, you can select specific printer options to control the print layout or the pages you want to be printed and the number of copies.

1. In the Navigation Pane, right-click the report that you want to print, and click **Print Preview**.
2. On the **Print Preview** tab, in the **Print** group, click **Print**.

3. Select your print options, and then click **OK** to print your report.

4.

To save paper, or to send a print job to a commercial printer, or send the report via e-mail, you can create a .pdf or .xps format of your report: On the **Print Preview** tab, in the **Data** group, click **PDF or XPS**.

PREVIEW BEFORE PRINTING

You can open a report in Print Preview by using one of the following methods:

- To preview a report that is not already open, in the Navigation Pane, right-click the report that you want to preview, and then click **Print Preview**.

  Alternatively, Click **File** > **Print**, and then click **Print Preview**.

Alternatively,If the report is open, right-click the document tab for the report, and then click **Print Preview**.

If you want to see several pages of the report, move to other pages, or view multiple pages at the same time when previewing you report, try any the following options:

- To magnify an area on the report, on the **Print Preview** tab, in the **Zoom** group, click the arrow below **Zoom** and select a magnification percentage. You can also use the Zoom control in the lower right-hand corner of your window.
- To preview multiple pages at a time, in the **Zoom** group, click **Two Pages** or click **More Pages** and then select an option.

  Select your print options: In the **Print** group, click **Print** and then select your print options.

  Close Print Preview: In the **Close Preview** group, click **Close Print Preview**.

CHAPTER 6. WHAT IS A MACRO?

A macro is a tool that allows you to automate tasks and add functionality to your forms, reports, and controls. For example, if you add a command button to a form, you associate the button's **OnClick** event to a macro, and the macro contains the commands that you want the button to perform each time it is clicked.

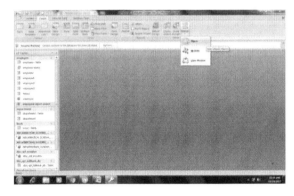

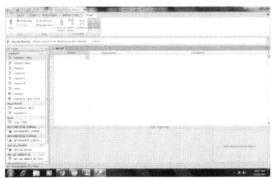

When you build a macro, you select each action from a drop-down list and then fill in the required information for each action. Macros enable you to add functionality to forms, reports, and controls without writing code in a Visual Basic for Applications (VBA) module. Macros provide a subset of the commands that are available in VBA, and most people find it easier to build a macro than to write VBA code

ARGUMENTS

An argument is a value that provides information to the action, such as what string to display in a message box, which control to operate on, and so on. Some arguments are required, and some others are optional. Arguments are visible in the **Action Arguments** pane at the bottom of the Macro Builder.

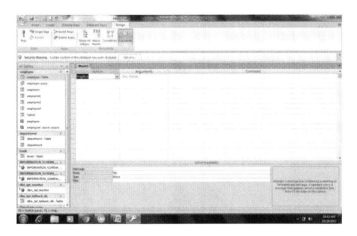

To display the **Arguments** column, click **Arguments** in the **Show/Hide** group on the **Design** tab.

CONDITIONS

A condition specifies certain criteria that must be met before an action will be performed. You can use any expression that evaluates to True/False or Yes/No. The action will not be executed if the expression evaluates to False, No, or 0 (zero). If the expression evaluates to any other value, the action will be run.

To display the **Conditions** column in the Macro Builder, on the **Design** tab, in the **Show/Hide** group, click **Conditions**.

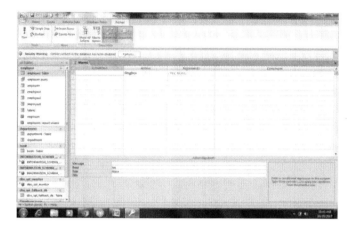

MACRO ACTIONS

Actions are the basic building blocks of macros. Access provides a large number of actions from which to choose, enabling a wide variety of commands. For example, some of the more commonly used actions can open a report, find a record, display a message box, or apply a filter to a form or report.

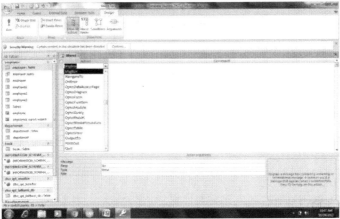

-
- **Error handling and debugging** Office Access 2007 provides new macro actions,
  including **OnError**(similar to the "On Error" statement in VBA)

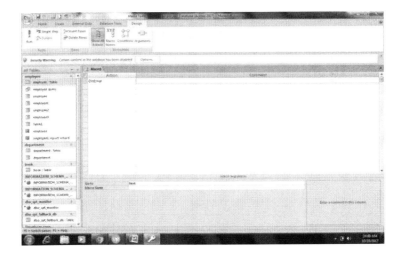

And **ClearMacroError**, which allow you to perform specific actions when errors occur while your macro is running. Also, the new **SingleStep** macro action allows you to enter single-step mode at any point in your macro so that you can observe how your macro works one action at a time.

Macro Builder features

You first open the Macro Builder, the **Action** column, the **Arguments** column, and the **Comment** column are displayed.

Under **Action Arguments**, you enter and edit arguments for each macro action, if any is required. A description box that gives you a short description of each action or argument is displayed. Click an action or action argument to read its description in the box.

Create an embedded macro

1. Open the form or report that will contain the macro in Design view or Layout view. To open a form or report, right-click it in the Navigation Pane, and then click **Design View** or **Layout View**.
2. If the property sheet is not already displayed, press F4 to display it.
3. Click the control or section that contains the event property in which you want to embed the macro.

   To select the entire form or report, click **Report** in the drop-down list at the top of the property sheet.

4. In the property sheet, click the **Event** tab.
5. Click the event property in which you want to embed the macro, and then click, next to the box.

6. In the **Choose Builder** dialog box, click **Macro Builder**, and then click **OK**.
7. In the Macro Builder, click in the first row of the **Action** column.
8. In the **Action** drop-down list, click the action you want.
9. Fill in any required arguments in the **Action Arguments** pane and then move to the next action row.
10. Repeat steps 8 and nine until your macro is complete.
11. Click **Save**, then click **Close**.

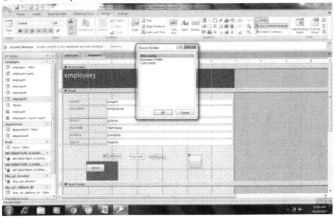

Run a macro directly

To run a macro directly, do one of the following:

- Navigate to the macro in the Navigation Pane, and then double-click the macro name.
- On the **Database Tools** tab, in the **Macro** group, click **Run Macro**, click the macro in the **Macro Name** list, and then click **OK**.

- If the macro is open in Design view, click **Run** on the **Design** tab, in the **Tools** group.

OTHER BOOKS BY (ANDREI BESEDIN)

1) **50 MOST POWERFUL EXCEL FUNCTIONS AND FORMULAS: ADVANCED WAYS TO SAVE YOUR TIME AND MAKE COMPLEX ANALYSIS QUICK AND EASY!**
   HTTPS://WWW.AMAZON.COM/MOST-POWERFUL-EXCEL-FUNCTIONS-FORMULAS/DP/1521549915/REF=ZG_BS_13 2559011_7?_ENCODING=UTF8&PSC=1&R EFRID=QT5D1NR6CBRAFTGEP7AG

2) **SECRETS OF LOOKUP: BECOME MORE PRODUCTIVE WITH VLOOKUP, FREE YOUR TIME!**
   HTTPS://WWW.AMAZON.COM/SECRETS-LOOKUP-PRODUCTIVE-VLOOKUP-TRAINING-EBOOK/DP/B073P4FVSG/REF=LA_B07211P1N S_1_10?S=BOOKS&IE=UTF8&QID=149952473 0&SR=1-10

3) **TOP 3 EXCEL FORMULAS AND FUNCTIONS**
   HTTPS://WWW.AMAZON.COM/EXCEL-FORMULAS-FUNCTIONS-TRAINING-BOOK-EBOOK/DP/B0738LF8LL/REF=SR_1_6?IE=UTF 8&QID=1499524945&SR=8-6&KEYWORDS=TOP+3+EXCEL

4) **AMAZING JAVA: LEARN JAVA QUICKLY!**
   https://www.amazon.com/Amazing-JAVA-Learn-Quickly-ebook/dp/B0737762M8/ref=la_B07211P1NS_1_2?s=

books&ie=UTF8&qid=1499524891&sr=1-2&refinements=p_82%3AB07211P1NS

5) **DASH DIET TO MAKE MIDDLE AGED PEOPLE HEALTHY AND FIT: 40 DELICIOUS RECIPES FOR PEOPLE OVER 40 YEARS OLD!**

https://www.amazon.com/Dash-Diet-Middle-People-Healthy-ebook/dp/B071WZBZPB/ref=la_B07211P1NS_1_3?s=books&ie=UTF8&qid=1499524891&sr=1-3&refinements=p_82%3AB07211P1NS

6) **MEDITERRANEAN DIET FOR MIDDLE AGED PEOPLE: 40 DELICIOUS RECIPES TO MAKE PEOPLE OVER 40 YEARS OLD HEALTHY AND FIT!**

https://www.amazon.com/Mediterranean-diet-middle-aged-people-ebook/dp/B0723952FH/ref=la_B07211P1NS_1_4?s=books&ie=UTF8&qid=1499524891&sr=1-4&refinements=p_82%3AB07211P1NS

7) **FITNESS FOR MIDDLE AGED PEOPLE: 40 POWERFUL EXERCISES TO MAKE PEOPLE OVER 40 YEARS OLD HEALTHY AND FIT!**

https://www.amazon.com/Fitness-Middle-Aged-People-Exercises-ebook/dp/B072VFBT99/ref=la_B07211P1NS_1_5?s=books&ie=UTF8&qid=1499524891&sr=1-5&refinements=p_82%3AB07211P1NS

8) **MARKET RESEARCH: GLOBAL MARKET FOR GERMANIUM AND GERMANIUM PRODUCTS**

https://www.amazon.com/Market-Research-Global-Germanium-Products-ebook/dp/B00X4JBM92/ref=la_B07211P1NS_1_9?s=books&ie=UTF8&qid=1499524891&sr=1-9&refinements=p_82%3AB07211P1NS

9) STOCKS, MUTUAL FUNDS:THE START UP GUIDE ON STOCK INVESTING

https://www.amazon.com/Stocks-Mutual-Funds-Start-Investing-ebook/dp/B00WOGXCDU/ref=la_B07211P1NS_1_6?s=books&ie=UTF8&qid=1499524891&sr=1-6&refinements=p_82%3AB07211P1NS

10) Aerobics, running & jogging: 30 Minutes a Day Burn Fat Workout for Middle Aged Men"!: Two most powerful ways to burn fat quickly!

https://www.amazon.com/Aerobics-running-jogging-Minutes-powerful-ebook/dp/B00WA9ESG6/ref=la_B07211P1NS_1_7?s=books&ie=UTF8&qid=1499524891&sr=1-7&refinements=p_82%3AB07211P1NS

11) Diamond Cut Six Packs: How To Develop Fantastic Abs

https://www.amazon.com/Diamond-Cut-Six-Packs-Fantastic-ebook/dp/B01E2OELVS/ref=la_B07211P1NS_1_8?s=books&ie=UTF8&qid=1499524891&sr=1-8&refinements=p_82%3AB07211P1NS

12) 15 MOST POWERFUL FEATURES OF PIVOT TABLES!: Save Your Time With MS Excel!

https://www.amazon.com/MOST-POWERFUL-FEATURES-PIVOT-TABLES-ebook/dp/B074THF418/ref=sr_1_3?ie=UTF8&qid=1504594835&sr=8-3&keywords=besedin

13) 20 Most Powerful Excel Conditional Formatting Techniques!: Save Your Time With MS Excel

https://www.amazon.com/Powerful-Excel-Conditional-Formatting-Techniques-ebook/dp/B074H9W6XJ/ref=sr_1_4?ie=UTF8&qid=1504594835&sr=8-4&keywords=besedin

14) Secrets of MS Excel VBA/Macros for Beginners: Save Your Time With Visual Basic Macros!

https://www.amazon.com/Secrets-Excel-VBA-Macros-Beginners-ebook/dp/B075GYBLWT/ref=sr_1_7?ie=UTF8&qid=1506057725&sr=8-7&keywords=besedin

15) Secrets of Business Plan Writing: Business Plan Template and Financial Model Included!

https://www.amazon.com/Secrets-Business-Plan-Writing-Financial-ebook/dp/B076GJK8T1/ref=sr_1_9?ie=UTF8&qid=1509858352&sr=8-9&keywords=besedin

THANK YOU BUT CAN I ASK YOU FOR A FAVOR?

Let me say thank you for downloading and reading my book. This would be all about Access in this book. Hope you enjoyed it but you need to keep on learning to be perfect!If you enjoyed this book, found it useful or otherwise then I'd reallygrateful it if you would post a short review on Amazon. I read all the reviews personally so I can get your feedback and make this book even better.

Thanks for your support!

53388977R10104

Made in the USA
Middletown, DE
28 November 2017